MINING BETWEEN CERES AND ST ANDREWS

WINDFALL BOOKS

D1437829

JOHN MCMANUS

SCHOOL OF GEOGRAPHY AND GEOSCIENCES
UNIVERSITY OF ST ANDREWS

© 2010

Edited by Lillian King

Cover design by Belle Hammond
Original cover picture by kind permission of Newtongrange Mining museum
Typesetting, layout and design by Windfall Books
Published by Windfall Books, Kelty
01383 831076
windfallbooks@tiscali.co.uk
www.windfallbooks.co.uk

ISBN No: 978 0 9557264 8 4

ABOUT THE AUTHOR

John McManus was born in Harwich, Essex, and educated in the local County High School followed by six years at Imperial College, University of London, where he studied Geology in the Royal School of Mines (1958-1963), graduating with BSc and PhD degrees. He lectured in Queen's College, Dundee, later the University of Dundee, before transferring to the University of St Andrews where he became Professor. A Fellow of the Royal Society of Edinburgh, he has published over 200 scientific articles. A former President of the international Estuarine and Coastal Sciences Association, John has served on Natural Environment Research Council committees, Boards of the Scottish Natural Heritage and Scottish Environment Protection Agency and has represented UK at UNESCO. He enjoys an active musical life, and sings with the East Fife Male Voice Choir, having been President of the Cupar Opera Company and also of the Cupar Choral Association.

FOREWORD

It comes as a surprise to visitors and to many local residents to learn that the northeast of Fife was a centre of considerable coal mining activity for well over a hundred years during the eighteenth and nineteenth centuries and for probably many years before that. Whole families were involved in the many enterprises, with wives and children working as integral parts of teams alongside their husbands and fathers. Very long hours, often more than twelve hours each day except the Sabbath would be worked below ground, and collier families were commonly regarded as some form of sub-species of humans by the rest of the populace.

The aim of this contribution is not to chronicle the hardships, or the complexities of social history involved, but to examine the physical constraints imposed by the geological structures, the geographical distribution of the coal seams and the difficulties encountered in attempting to exploit the mineral wealth of the area. Each coalfield site was beset with specific sets of problems controlled by the geological setting, and these determined the manner of workings which were possible at each locality. Inevitably, with the passage of time the records differ in their degree of completeness, so that, for example, the stories of the Ceres, Callange and Drumcarro mines are much more complete than those from farther east, where the workings were often earlier.

The nature of each of the coalfields is addressed in turn, bringing together the facts that can be drawn from the reports of mining engineers and geologists, but often using additional material from parish records and local newspapers. Where possible, attention is drawn to the remnant evidence which may still be recognised today. All of the sites referred to are of reasonably easy access, and may be reached from the public roads. However, it must be stressed that permission should be sought from landowners and farmers before any attempt is made to enter property. Some farm fields traditionally host excitable bulls, and most others will be active sites for growing crops. Some of the long-abandoned pit shafts may not be totally secure and, almost every year, at least one of these structures collapses, usually, but not always, under the wheels of vehicles such as tractors tilling the fields. It would be foolhardy to attempt to enter old workings without very adequate precautions, and never alone without specific permission.

This account was begun after I retired, and I was very fortunate to have been encouraged to complete the work by my late and deeply missed wife, Barbara. I wish to thank the many people who have generously given time, advice and shared local knowledge. Others, mostly not geologically trained, have kindly agreed to read through early versions of the manuscript in an attempt to ensure that I have made the material accessible to the general reader. I am indebted to landowners, farmers, local residents; staff in The Coal Authority, National Mining Museum in Mansfield; from the libraries of the British Geological Survey (Edinburgh) and the University of St Andrews; and especially to Captain Ivor Bayliss, Professor David Williams, and Dr Kay Smith for their critical comments during text preparation. I am extremely grateful for the most welcome assistance given by Lillian King and Belle Hammond in the tasks of editing the text and preparing the cover illustrations.

Mr. G. F. Sandeman, Senior Cartographer in the School of Geography and Geosciences at the University of St Andrews, produced the text figures and Neil McManus kindly provided photographs and tidied the tables and plates of the early mine plans. These invaluable assistants are in no way responsible for any errors which may remain. For these I take full responsibility, and offer my apologies in advance. However, as each of the mines was closed before 1900, I rest assured that no former collier who worked at the industrial sites discussed will come forward to contradict my interpretations on the basis of first hand experience. Nevertheless I would be most grateful to learn of any further information which may be available in family diaries, journals or legends from the local mining communities.

John McManus

Dedicated to the memory of Barbara, my loving wife of forty-two years, an outstanding mother and inspirational musician.

INTRODUCTION

The coalfields of Fife have long played an important part in the economic development of the region. In particular, the coal played a prominent role as a fuel for growth of manufacturing during the industrial revolution. Later it was used to power the railway transport system throughout the country, and more recently as an energy source for electricity generation. The more senior members of the present population will have memories of the concentrations of coal workings in central and west Fife, but in the early days of coal extraction many small pits and mines operated throughout the kingdom, including in the North-east of Fife. Today there is little to be seen to remind the resident or visitor of this industrial past, but records exist of numerous, often short-lived workings which provided employment for collier families. We should not forget that many of these families were seen as part of the collieries and were bought and sold with the properties when they changed hands. Others, owned by the estates, divided their time between mining in the winter and agricultural activities in the summer months.

The nature of the coal workings evolved through time, from simple excavations in valley sides or coastal cliffs, through systems of mines creating hand cut rooms with intervening coal pillars left to support the roofs. The more modern patterns of coal extraction, or winning, involve the use of powered cutting equipment in the highly economical longwall workings. The details of how, when, and where the coals were won from the ground, and the conditions under which the colliers lived and worked are largely forgotten today. In this account I will endeavour to remind the reader of the hardships and hazards faced on a daily basis by the many early underground miners, including their children.

Although records of the early mining operations in Fife are far from complete, many documents in the Fife Archives relate to some of the estates which grew in prosperity as the coals were exploited. Elsewhere, the Scottish Records Office in Edinburgh holds many further instructive documents relating to dealings with mining engineers and financing of the enterprises. Local newspapers from the eighteenth century onwards contain records of new findings, borehole exploration and comments on production, before the inevitable closure notices and advertisements of displenishment sales as the workings were abandoned.

Where relevant misdemeanours occurred, the minutes of Kirk Sessions are also useful sources of information. Fortunately, when nationalisation took place in 1947, the National Coal Board appointed experienced mining engineers to track down what mining records remained, and their hand-written summaries of information extending back into the mid-1700s provide invaluable information on the opening, working and often of the closing of the mines.

The detailed economic accounts by S.B. Forbes (1955) derived from records in the National Coal Board archives and also held in the archives of the British Geological Survey at Murchison House, Edinburgh, are particularly helpful in relation to the east of Fife. Unfortunately, the legal requirement for the production and submission of mine abandonment plans was not introduced until 1890, so the detail of workings in the early days of the industry have largely been lost. Only very limited records of the early workings in Fife are held by the National Mining Museum in Mansfield or in the library of the Scottish Mining Museum at Newtongrange, Edinburgh.

It is strongly recommended that in exploring the area the Ordnance Survey maps at a scale of 1:25000, sheets 370 (Glenrothes North, Falkland & Lomond Hills), and Sheet 371 (St Andrews & East Fife) should be used. The geological maps of the British Geological Survey, Edinburgh, which cover the areas concerned are 1:50,000 scale sheets 49 (Arbroath) and 41, (North Berwick).

The broad agricultural valley leading eastwards from the village of Ceres towards Pitscottie is drained by the Ceres Burn. From Pitscottie. the waters flow to the North Sea by way of the Dura Den gorge and the River Eden. Further east, the Kinness Burn and its southern tributaries flow directly into the sea at St Andrews. Separating the two drainage basins is an area of relatively high ground, bounded to the north by the Blebo Craigs ridge and to the south by the Ladeddie-Drumcarrow ridge.

Whilst today the area projects an almost uniform air of peaceful and prosperous arable farming, in the eighteenth and nineteenth centuries mining for coal, limestone, and also for ironstone was practised in many parts alongside the agricultural activity. Records of local exploitation of coals in the earliest days are few and far between, but written records of the mining near Ceres from 1749 onwards exist, in the form of an accounts book, currently lodged in Cupar Library. From several early eye-sketch plans it is known that by the mid-eighteenth century the coals underlying much of the hillside to the east of Ceres had already been removed, and the old workings abandoned.

Although there was no requirement for the production of mine abandonment plans before the 1890s, some records remain of the mining from about 1750 onwards, and we know that the extraction of the coals gradually extended eastwards, so that the Callange mines, which operated from the late seventeenth century were active until the early nineteenth century. Further east coals were taken from the south side of Drumcarrow Hill, where the mines were active until 1850, and the slightly later Ladeddie operations until 1863. By this time the Craigton Common, Winthank and Denhead workings were also coming to an end, but the gas coal mines of the Denork and Claremont estates continued in operation until the late 1880s. The renowned Blackband Ironstone and associated coal workings at Denhead and in its near vicinity were in operation during the 1840s and 1850s. The last working coal mines, albeit to the south of the area to be addressed, were at Newbigging of Craighall and Peat Inn, Drumhead both lasting till 1907.

FORMATION OF COALS

For perhaps 4000 million years the earth's surface was free from plant life, and therefore free from insects and animals such as early amphibians and reptiles, which would have been dependent on plants for their food. Not so beneath the seas where, possibly from quite early times, primitive organisms lived in the waters, enjoying increasingly complex lives, before developing into plants and animals, and eventually, somewhere between 700 and 600 million years ago, starting to secrete hard skeletal material which enabled their remains to become readily preserved and recognised as fossils.

A huge variety of creatures lived in the early seas, but it was not until about 420 million years ago that plants began to extend inland from the sea, almost certainly along the shores of coastal estuaries and along the rivers. This migration, and the necessary adaptation to life in freshwater put great chemical and physical demands on the plants as they colonised the new environments which they were meeting. The land surface across much of what would become Europe and North America, towards the start of the geological period known as the Devonian, was essentially of barren, bare rock. A line of volcanoes extended eastward from Stirling and along the northern margins of Fife, to Tayport. The spectacular lava and ash producing volcanic activity was brought to an end by a mid-Devonian phase of mountain building about 390 million years ago. This orogenic activity served to lift the Grampian mountains and allow the formation of powerful southward flowing rivers which carried sediments in the form of silts, sands and gravels, materials eroded from the northern high ground. In the lowlands to the south these sediments were deposited, burying many of the newly arrived plants which were still concentrated along the estuaries and river banks, The remains of some of these fragile plants, which were to form some of the first fossils of land-living organisms, are occasionally found in sandstones on the shore of the Tay estuary near Wormit.

During the 50-60 million years of the Devonian Period, the plants underwent considerable diversification, becoming thoroughly adapted to the demands of their new, relatively dry surroundings, with freshwaters lacking in salt. In general, water drains rapidly from banks of sand and gravel so that, away from the rivers and valley bottoms, essentially dry conditions prevailed. Once buried beneath dried out flood deposits, the remains of the plants became readily oxidised, the carbon combining with the oxygen to form the gas carbon dioxide, so that their fibrous structures often faded away, only rarely leaving more than fragile traces of their former existence. Towards the end of the Devonian period there was a substantial change in the climatic conditions as the European-North American landmass continued to drift northwards, within the southern hemisphere, i.e. towards the equator. As the rains increased the plants began to proliferate, and the land surfaces eventually became covered with lush vegetation, developing what would have been jungles and rainforests, similar to those of the tropics today, although with more primitive plant forms. We know from the evidence of rock-magnetism that the Europe-American land mass occupied a position within the equatorial belt during the succeeding Carboniferous Period.

What was this land like in Carboniferous times? A large river system flowed across Fife from the northeastern mountains on to broad coastal plains which were bordered by shallow, warm seas. There were certainly extensive coastal plains on which grew swathes of different forms of plants arranged according to their needs for water and nutrients. Tall tree-like lycopods such as Stigmaria and Lepidodendron reached up to thirty metres and more in height. Around the base of similarly sized horsetails like Calamites, was undergrowth with small ferns of many varieties. The sediments carried by the rivers built up deltas where they entered the seas, and the sands and muds also spread out along the coasts, aided by the tidal currents. Within and between the deltas there were extensive, often stagnant swampy lagoons and coastal inlets. Insects of many sorts, including giant millipedes, cockroaches and primitive dragon-flies, are known to have lived in the swamps. Offshore in the shallow coastal waters organisms such as corals, the lamp-shelled brachiopods, and sea-lilies (crinoids) crowded together creating reef-like barriers landward of which muddy lagoons formed where floating plants and plankton thrived, their decaying organic matter later giving rise to deposits of productive oil shales.

The layered rocks within which the coal seams of North East Fife are found were deposited during the central part of the Carboniferous or early Namurian period, some 328-322 million years ago. The sediments supplied by rivers flowing southwestwards into the coastal waters were normally laid down in such a way that the larger particles, the sands, became deposited relatively close to the river mouths and shorelines, and progressively finer grained deposits of silts and muds were carried into the deeper waters or more remote sites. The accumulating material gradually built forward, so that the muds became overlain by layers of silt and those in turn by sands. In this way a succession was formed in which the material gradually became coarser upwards as the shoreline advanced seawards. Eventually sand banks emerged above normal water level and the ever opportunistic plants took root as the coastal forests extended seaward from the former shorelines. This pattern was related to the formation of deltas and accreting coastlines during times of stable or gradually falling sea level, each creating a mass of materials usually ten to thirty metres thick.

Away to the south, in the circum-polar regions of the day, repeated cycles of glaciation were occurring. During the cold periods, as ice-sheets built up, the water was withdrawn from the oceans, sea levels fell world wide and coastal plains became drained. Nearshore sediment banks would have gradually emerged above the waters and been subject to the rapid colonisation by plants, leading to expansion of the forests towards the retreating sea. From place to place drainage channels would have formed cutting through the peaty forest floors and into the underlying layers of soft sediment.

Later, during the warmer parts of the climate cycles, as refrigeration decreased around the poles the melting waters were returned to the seas and world wide sea levels rose swiftly, swamping the newly forested coastal plains, burying them beneath fresh sediments deposited from the open coastal waters. Sometimes these sediments took the form of limestones, sitting directly upon the peats, but more often it was the muds and silts which were the next set of materials to be deposited. The result was repetition of inundation and emergence of the land surface on a global scale at intervals of around 100,000 years. There was ample time for the plant migrations to occur within such intervals.

In Fife, the St Monance Brecciated Limestone marks the base of the Lower Limestone Formation, and the Upper Kinniny Limestone marks the base of the Limestone Coal

Formation. This gives the proper titles to the groups of rocks in which the coals of North East Fife are found. The nature of the environments in which the sediments were laid down is reflected by the fossils of organisms whose remains were entrapped in them. So we may identify marine fossils, corals, shell-fish and crinoids or relatively freshwater creatures such as water fleas and non-marine types of shell-fish, often in abundance in the different layers of the succession of sediments. Deposition of the upward coarsening successions of sediments was repeated many times, with more than thirty repetitions recorded locally.

During the life of the forests, as individual plants died and their trunks and stems collapsed, the wood, twigs and leaves fell into the waters around the bases of the plants. The presence of stagnant pools of oxygen-depleted water in lakes or on the jungle floor ensured that oxidation was not possible for the fallen plant materials so that only partial decay took place. This ensured the survival of the carbon fixed into their cells from the soils and atmospheric gases during the life of the plants. Within the largely static waters the plant fragments remained in place in the water-logged environment, ultimately generating a layer of peat upon which fresh plants would have grown, before also contributing their wastes to the accumulation. As further materials built up through time, the peat layers became progressively thicker.

When the patterns of coastal change led to sands, muds or limestones being deposited above the peat, the weight of these sediments gradually compressed the peat, squeezing out the waters between the plant remains. As progressively more and more sediments built up above the initial peat, so the layer became slowly transformed into a layer of brown coal. This in turn suffered further burial and a combination of pressure and heat due to the burial converted the layer into what we recognise as black bituminous coal. Today the actual coal seams are about one tenth of the thickness of the original peat deposit. It is useful to bear this fact in mind when reading of seams 2.5–4m in thickness, which would have needed some considerable time for their original peats, then 25–40m thick to develop.

To gain an appreciation of exactly what a coal seam looks like, one of the easiest sites to visit is the sea-cliff between the Sea-Life Centre, by the Step Rock swimming pool and the castle at St Andrews. At any stage other than high tide the cliff-foot platform and beach provides ready access to what appear to be horizontally distributed layers of rock, mainly consisting of sandstones. Within the visible succession are several thin black coal seams. Above the cliff-foot concrete protective wall, the lowest and most accessible coal sits upon a former soil layer through which fossil rootlets and occasionally trunks from the original plants may be seen. Other thin coals also occur towards the upper parts of the cliff but no attempt should be made to collect specimens of the coals or scale the cliffs. A short way along the foot of the cliff a small inlet reveals that the layering is not in fact horizontal, but is inclined into the cliff at an appreciable angle. This is quite normal throughout the local coalfields. As we will see later, underground access to the coals would normally be by way of a shaft to the coal seam and thereafter along the horizontal direction, working the coals up the slope, from and above the access roadway. Following this seam downwards would soon lead to the level of standing water within the rocks.

Preserved in the frequently repeated successions of rock types, the former organisms now seen as fossils, were undergoing modification, with gradual evolution of early species into later more advanced relatives. This form of change is recognised in both the marine and non-marine creatures. Indeed because of the economic importance of knowing where in a particular sequence of sedimentary rocks a particular coal seam is to be found, there have been many studies of the evolution of the plants, corals and both marine and non-marine shell-fish during the Carboniferous period.

Using the evidence from fossils, the individual coal seams may be traced across huge distances throughout Britain and into Europe and even North America, which was a near neighbour until the North Atlantic opened more than 200 million years later. There were local differences in the thickness of the seams, depending on local rates of land subsidence, but the patterns in the successions of deposited rocks are readily detected.

In Fife, the coals predominantly formed during two parts of the Carboniferous, the early ones deposited between 328 and 322 million years ago, found in the east and west of Fife, are some of the earliest worked anywhere in the world (those of Spitzbergen are slightly older). They mostly pre-date the coals of England and Wales, where the geography of the times consisted mainly of rather deeper water marine conditions, characterised by accumulation of limestones. These were deposited across Central Scotland from time to time, marking the brief periods of relatively high sea level, but here they are rarely more than a few metres thick. The younger coals of Fife, deposited between 313 and 308 million years ago, occur in the Wemyss-Dysart and Westfield areas and were deposited at the same time as many of the coals of England and Wales. During the time that the long term pattern of global sea level changes occurred in Scotland there were local episodes of volcanic activity, leading to the formation of features such as the Arthur's Seat and Castle rock volcanoes of Edinburgh, the Largo Law, Lomond Hills and over a hundred more smaller vents in Fife. Local uplifts and depressions of the land occurred at many times during the early Carboniferous, and these local crustal movements allowed basins to develop, in which individual coal seams became much thicker than in adjacent relatively high areas, where several thin seams may have been deposited during the same time period. Of the many coal seams relatively few were sufficiently thick to allow extraction to take place. Records show that coals thinner than forty five centimetres were rarely worked. Even within the Ceres area, where no less than seventeen seams are recorded, we know of only six or seven that were actually worked to any great extent.

COAL MINING HISTORY AND METHODS

The story of coal exploitation is a long and complex one, linking technological advance, social history and international economic changes. The increasing ability of the miners to penetrate ever deeper into the earth to ply their craft had an accompaniment of problems of disposing of extracted but unwanted materials. For convenience the evolution of the industry will be addressed as a series of temporally linked changes.

Before 1500

It is known that during the Roman occupation of Britain the coals along the sea coasts and river banks were exploited by forces occupying the Antonine Wall, in the second century AD. This 60km long clay or turf-based defensive wall stretched between the Clyde at Old Kilpatrick and the Forth at Carriden, (Montgomery, 1994). The coals were used by the Roman blacksmiths and also for cremations. Whether they were used to heat the hypocaust systems beneath the major houses is not known. We do not know whether the Romans brought the technology of coal use with them or whether perhaps they learned its use from the indigenous peoples. The Romans withdrew from Britain late in the fourth century AD, and four hundred years later the Venerable Bede wrote that coals were no longer being burnt, (Galloway, 1882).

The documented history of coal winning in Scotland goes back only to the twelfth century, when King Malcolm IV (1153-65) and King David I affirmed their right to take a tithe of the coals recovered, presumably for burning in their stone-built castles. It was far too dangerous to use for heating in the vernacular thatch-roofed wooden houses of the time.

About 1202, William de Vipont granted a tithe of his coals from Carriden to the monks of Holyrood. In two later charters, dated 1210 and 1219, Seyer de Quinci granted the monks of Newbattle Abbey a coal works and quarry near Tranent, (McKechnie and Macgregor, 1958). This implied that at least surface mining was already taking place, and a charter dated 1291 was issued to the monks of Dunfermline Abbey, permitting them to work the coals within the Pittencreiff Estate, including Calurig, now Gallowrig, (McManus, 2008) for their own use, but not for sale to others, (Cochran-Patrick, 1878, Cunningham, 1913). In 1294, the monks of Paisley Abbey were given rights to dig sea-coal, a term which was applied to all coals at that time, not just to those from the coast. That same year an Act of the Scottish Parliament was passed to regulate the sale of coal from Berwick-upon-Tweed on the pretext that it was becoming scarce. However, by this time coal was already being used for heating in monasteries and castles but less so by the general population even where it was available.

In 1306 a Royal Proclamation was made in London, effectively the first Clean Air Act, banning the use of coal for domestic purposes in London in the belief that the smoke and fumes were dangerous to health. It is worth pointing out that by that time few of the wooden, thatch roofed houses had brick or stone built chimneys, and relied on smoke, usually from wood burning or peat fires, exiting either through open windows, doors or holes in the roofing. Coals were used at this time in the production of salt from the boiling off and evaporation of sea water in salt-pans, giving rise to place names such as Prestonpans, Kennetpans, Grangepans, The Pans and Pan Haven at Crail, Pans Goat by St Monans, Panhall at Dysart and at many other coastal sites. At Wemyss, in Fife, estate records show that salt production was active in 1428, (Moodie, 2002). According to the quality of the coals between six and sixteen tons of coal were needed to produce one ton of salt, (Duckham, 1970, Brotchie, 1998). By the mid-fourteenth century, most of the shallow near surface coal heughs or excavations were nearing exhaustion.

The mining industry that we would recognise today began to develop fully in the fifteenth century, by extending from quarrying of individual coal seams from outcrops along valley sides or at the coast, following the layers into the hillsides or cliffs to release the coals. Once the coals were removed the roof was supported on wooden props or by waste rocks which had been displaced as they were undercut. Penetration beneath the hillsides was commonly accompanied by the mine encountering the groundwater, the drainage of which became a major problem. Where the seams sloped upwards away from the valley side outcrop the waters would drain towards the entrance, under gravity, and extraction of the coal could continue with little hindrance.

However, where the seams were inclined downwards from valley side outcrop, if no means of removal of the water could be devised, the mining would cease soon after penetrating the water table into the saturated materials. The creation of a subsidiary, but crucial, tunnel, the day level, to collect the water and lead it away and downwards to a nearby valley floor could enable working to continue. (Fig.1)

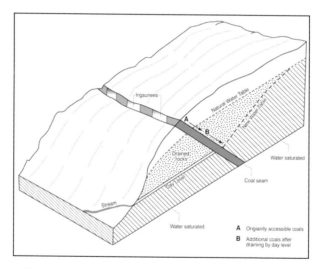

Fig.1. Original workings gave access to coals in section A, above the natural water table. Construction of the day level tunnel to lower the water table provided access to coals in section B

The miner could work only in the level free zone, i.e. above the level of the water table, unless this form of drainage was introduced. The outfalls from several of important day levels may still be seen at several sites in NE Fife, notably above Kinninmonth Bridge, between Pitscottie and Calange Farm.

Drift mines were driven directly from the surface along the coal seam. The near-horizontal entrance tunnels are known as adits, and their open entrances on the valley sides are still often referred to as ingaunees. Landscape features from the shallow near-surface workings are difficult to detect, because today they consist of little more than a sharp local increase in the slope across the outcrop of the worked seam, and are hard to recognise when vegetation-covered. The surface manifestations of the early workings are generally difficult to spot. Little unnecessary waste was carried from the workings and most of this goaf (rock fragments and fine coal dust) and small coals was retained within the mine to prevent or limit roof fall. All transport of material to the surface was by human labour and unnecessary expenditure of energy was to be avoided. In general only the great coals, large blocks of coal, and fist-sized lumps were carried to the surface, from where they could be sold in the markets or exported. Roughly one third of the hewed coal broke into small fragments, of little value unless the mine was near the sea and suitable salt pan or limestone workings, which could make use of the small or poor quality coals. However, in some localities, wastes derived from seam roof collapse or from layers of sandstone within the seams, were deposited on valley sides below the workings The First Statistical Account of Dysart, (Muirhead 1792), refers to a 'continuous line of waste visible for three miles along the crop.' Locally a landscape impact remained for many years after active outcrop or crop working had ceased (Bennett, 1978).

Away from the valley-side outcrops, where the seams lay at no great depth, the extraction of coal was made possible by the sinking of vertical shafts to the seams. The coals were removed from the immediate area at the base of the pit shaft, with roof supports where possible. These workings initially reached for short distances from the shaft base, the broadening along the coal seam, giving rise to their name as bell pits. (Fig 2)

Later many of the workings extended radially for over 50m as confidence in roofing supports increased. Occasionally the shafts penetrated more than one layer of coal and simultaneous working at two or more levels was possible. The coals were pulled to the base of the shaft in tubs by putters or drawers (children or women), and physically carried up the 15-25m to the surface by bearers, usually women, ascending sequences of ladders or stairs. Little waste from within the coals would have been brought to the surface, lest the load be rejected and the hewer effectively fined by surface quality control personnel. The use of bell-pits continued well into the eighteenth century. Similar pit shafts were used to carry coals to the surface where the seams were worked following a horizontal path within the coal and up the dip from the level in the coal seam. This marked an advance in the method of excavation and was possible where the seam could be connected to a day level drain. A line of shafts was created, each put down to the level within the seam and spaced at intervals which marked the progress of the removal of the coals. Accounting records from the Banfield Coalbook (1749-1761) show that in that one field, near Ceres, new shafts 40-50m deep were sunk every six months or so. Often the adjacent workings were deliberately connected to earlier excavations for the purposes of improving ventilation.

However, most abandoned shafts were filled with waste materials derived from the new shafts as they were constructed, but the presence of occasional hollows in the landscape above former workings testify to the fact that the back-filling was far from totally effective. A fine example of two such collapsed shafts is presently visible in fields of the Drumcarrow Equitage Centre. Other shaft tops are visible in the broken ground between Drumcarrow Craig and the Strathkinness to Colinsburgh road.

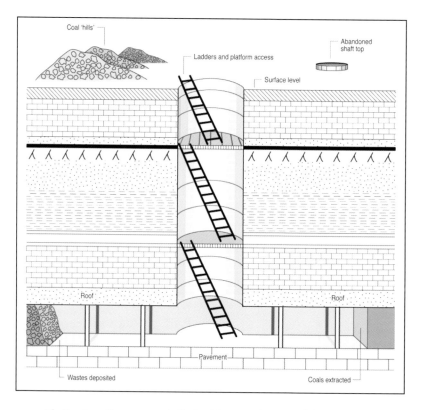

Fig.2. A section across a bell pit with access by way of three ladders. The coals were worked radially from the shaft base, with waste materials being left behind. Wooden props supported the roof above the coal seam

The total annual Scottish coal production at the start of the sixteenth century was less than 40,000 tons, so none of the many mines was large or highly productive, (McKechnie & Macgregor, 1958). The church was still collecting tithes from the colliers, with George, Archdean of St. Andrews and Commendator of Dunfermline Monastery in 1555 requiring that every ninth load of coal from the lands of Stentoun be paid as a feu to the convent. In many instances, the tacksmen operating the mines on private estates paid a tenth of the produce to the estate for the rent of the coal workings.

Most of the outcropping coal had been worked out by the end of the sixteenth century, as recorded for the Balgonie estate in central Fife, (Brodie, 1978). Once again there were real worries that the supply of coal would run out, and to protect local interests its export was again banned in 1563. A later Parliamentary Act of 1584 deemed that setting fire to coal heughs was a treasonable crime, and soon after that miner John Henry was hanged in Edinburgh for precisely this action.

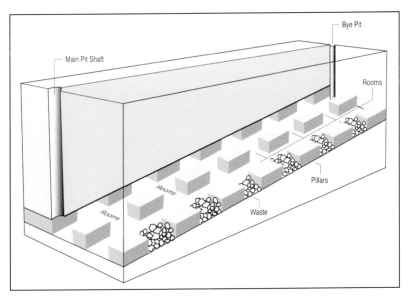

Fig.3. Illustration of 'stoop and room' or 'pillar and stall'
method of extraction. Much coal was left in place to
support the roof of the workings

The survival of the industry was assured when at the end of the sixteenth century the stoop and room, sometimes known as pillar and stall method of working was introduced to Scotland. This system of extraction, deliberately leaving blocks of the coal to serve as pillars supporting the roof of the seam while extraction continued around them, carried with it greater safety for the colliers and enabled them to push farther and farther underground from the access points In areas where the coals were near the surface this form of working could be applied in drift mines, but where access to the coals was by pit shafts the working customarily consisted of two shafts, the first of which reached the lowest level to be worked on the usually inclined seam.

From the base of this shaft, (the Deep Pit) a horizontal mine or road was constructed along the strike direction within the coal seam, for this was the working level which allowed any waters to drain to the day level tunnel. The working rooms were driven at right angles from the level, up the dip of the coal seam, together with a broader roadway up the dip to link with the base of a shallower shaft (the Bye Pit) formed at a high point of the workings. From the lower level road the colliers gradually worked up the slope, extracting rooms 3-5m square between which were left 2-4m square pillars of untouched coals to support the roof. (Fig.3)

In deeper mines, the rooms were no smaller but the pillars were thicker (often 8m square and more) to hold the additional weight of the super-incumbent rocks. By this method at best about two thirds of the coals were removed, (Duckham, 1970) the remainder being left in the supports. This minimised later subsidence, which would otherwise have been substantial from shallow workings. Some of the material removed during construction of the principal roads was taken to the surface, but, as coals were worked during the creation of the colliery, much of the waste material was packed into abandoned rooms. In many cases, as the workings were coming to an end, part or all of the pillars were removed in a systematic pattern, and the resultant permitted collapse, often extending to the surface, was complete within a decade or so.

Today it is possible to detect evidence of abandoned shallow depth stoop and room workings beneath many areas, as on slopes above the River Leven to the south of Markinch, Fife. Similar ground collapse marks former room and stoop workings in the small wood above the farm of Newbigging of Ceres. The systems of Deep and Bye Pits, levels and their associated workings are shown along the southern margins of the former Pittenweem Coalfield, in south-east Fife, on the 1785 map of Hogg, (Martin,1999) a site where Galloway (1895) estimated that 70% of the coal remained in the ground after the mining operations ceased. (Fig.4)

The deeply collapsed surface between the trees in the woods above the former coal road at Ceres may indicate abandoned shallow room and stoop workings, but elsewhere in North East Fife the coal seams are relatively steeply inclined so the shallow workings were very restricted in occurrence.

The second major phase of mining began in the mid-sixteenth century with the introduction of mechanised pumping methods to drain the waters from mine workings, thereby permitting extraction to be pushed to greater depths below ground. Hitherto, any drainage beyond the use of the day level had been by hand, using a dam and bailing system. The earliest of the new techniques was the sakhia, or Egyptian Wheel pump, whereby a horse follows a circular path around a central axle which drives a chain of buckets to scoop the water and transport it to the surface for discharge into a drainage channel and away to the nearest burn. Known as a horse engine, or gin for short, the system served to remove waters from the workings. There was no thought of lifting the coals to the surface by similar means until the 1670s. Sir George Bruce opened a shaft at Dunimarle, near Culross, and linked it to an artificially created island, dubbed the Moat Mine, by excavating beneath the Forth along the Jenny Peat seam. This mine, which was drained by horse engines, was overwhelmed during a major storm shortly after being famously visited in 1617 by King James I who briefly believed himself to have been kidnapped when he emerged on the island, (Montgomery, 1994). As early as 1622 at Wemyss in south Fife, a similar horse gin with a chain of leather buckets was used to drain workings from a shaft extending 40m below sea level under the Forth, (Moodie, 2002).

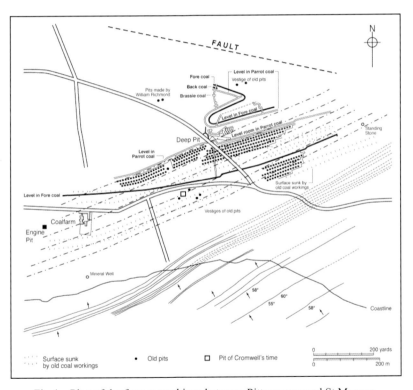

Fig.4. Plan of the former workings between Pittenweem and St Monans, after Galloway (1895). The residual coal pillars are indicated in black. The levels in the Fore Coal and Parrot Coal drained to 38 fathoms, the waters were raised at the Engine Pit, and discharged at the 'mineral well'

There was a steady export of both coals and salt from small harbours such as St Andrews where in 1655 Thomas Tucker, Cromwell's Commissioner to Scotland, was writing to say that many persons were employed as dockers at that harbour.

It was a short step from using horse power to introducing water- or wind-powered drainage methods, and many lades or diverted stream systems produced in the mid-seventeenth century survive today, although no longer providing power for industry. Nevertheless the water powered systems could work only during wet weather, and not in dry or freezing conditions, in the same way that wind powered systems could operate only during windy weather and therefore lacked reliability. Horse power was required to provide back-up for both of these methods. In the Ceres to St Andrews area there are few streams in the coalfields and none with sufficient power to drive the necessary water extraction systems. In Dura Den, water powered no less than five fabric or saw mills but they were dependent upon the waters of the Ceres Burn, which by-passed the coal workings on the hills to the south.

Major advances in the coal industry came with the introduction of steam-powered pumps by Savery (1698) and Newcomen (1705), first recorded in Scotland in 1720 at Elphinstone, near Airth, Stirlingshire and in 1725 in Midlothian. These early 'fire-engines' used coals to raise the steam, but for some time they were regarded with suspicion and considered unreliable. Precision engineering of the equipment was lacking and occasionally the boilers are reported to have exploded during use. Production from the Scottish mines was still small, and the economic depression with which the eighteenth century opened did little to revitalise the industry despite the opening of market access to the New World after the Treaty of Union in 1707.

Up until this time there was relatively little waste produced from the mines. Only marketable material was carried to the surface and the goaves or wastes were packed into the excavated areas below ground. The newly introduced steam engines required the burning of coal and the consequent production of ash, which again was buried within the abandoned areas of the workings, for the engines were normally situated below ground. A by-product of the location of the engines near the base of the shaft was that heated air was released into the shaft, and as it rose so it drew in cooler air down the more remote ventilation shafts, so improving the quality of air for the colliers and expelling unwanted, sometimes explosive gases from the workings.

1750-1850

A huge transformation in the coal industry was experienced in Scotland after 1750, when the impact of the industrial revolution was first felt. By 1750, it is estimated that on average annual coal consumption was between 0.5 and 0.75 tons per head of the population, (Duckham, 1970). Peat was still cut and burned in many areas. Beyond the mines, the development of iron smelting using coke to obtain higher temperatures in the furnaces of the Carron Ironworks and others in 1759, led to greatly increased demand for the supply of coal. The coke was produced by heating the coals to release the gases, producing a porous-textured, light weight fuel which when heated in a draught was capable of yielding sufficiently high temperatures to melt the ores. Many new and deeper mines were created.

Into this situation came James Watt who observed substantial wastage of steam in the 'atmospheric' Newcomen engine, which gave a discontinuous output of power surges, and in 1763 he developed a double acting cylinder system, which enabled a shaft to be rotated continually. A flywheel on the shaft could be used to drive machinery such as pumps and winding wheels. This opened up endless possibilities for the mining industry, and steam engines were introduced at the Kinneil Colliery, West Lothian, in 1768, primarily for use in pumping, but it was not until after 1784 that their use as winding engines was introduced to carry the coals up to the surface from the foot of the shaft. This led to a reduction in the need for direct labour in the haulage of the coals. The use of mechanical power also made it easier to enlarge the mine roadways below ground. Initially wooden, but later iron rails were installed to speed the transport of the coal tubs to the shaft foot, and soon thereafter the first pit ponies were taken below ground to haul the coal tubs to the shaft foot.

There is no indication that animal power was used in the mines of eastern Fife, although they were present in both the Dysart workings and those at Dunfermline at the time of the First Statistical Account. The opening of the underground roads produced excess wastes which could not be accommodated in abandoned workings and these materials were transported to the surface for disposal.

At this time the recruitment of miners from Shropshire led to the introduction of a new method of working the coals, and this longwall exploitation became widely used, a technique which survives to the present day. In this method two tunnels 100-200m apart are driven into the coal seam from a shaft access road, and a tunnel linking them is formed. The down slope side of this tunnel is the longwall working face. The coal is removed from this face which is progressively moved down the slope towards the horizontal shaft access road. (Fig.5) Aided by gravity the coals are removed downwards to the normally much larger access tunnels, which are firmly supported by coal and rock walls or props. The roof of the area within which the miners work is supported on pit props which are moved forward as the face is cut away. Any wastes are packed into the abandoned areas from which the roof supports are moved forward and the roof of the sector from which the coals have been removed is allowed to collapse behind the workings. By such a method the entire thickness of the coal seam is removed, whereas previously only the thicker seams were worked, usually beneath a coal layer left behind as a roof over the workings. By this method it is also possible to work some of the thinner seams in the succession. A similar longwall working may be created to the rise between the two bounding tunnels as they extend away from the main access road into the working panel, with the collapse again behind the working face. The economics of such workings are greatly superior to the room and stoop method if the system can be used. However, because the entire seam thickness could now be extracted, there was commonly greater risk of damage to the land surface above the workings if shallow. The deployment of wastes below ground during production became a skilled task, but during the early phases of mine development substantial quantities of wastes were produced, and these were taken to the surface to accumulate as the earliest bings.

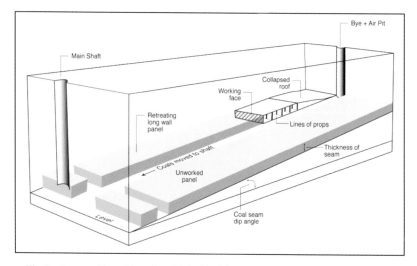

Fig.5. Longwall working, in which all of the coals are progressively removed, and as the working face retreats down slope the roof undergoes controlled collapse as hydraulic props are sequentially removed

Within the mines the increased use of steam driven power systems enabled large winding wheels to be used to lift the coals to the surface. When the early hemp ropes were replaced by steel wires for haulage in the mine roads and shafts after 1829, the transport of materials from below ground to the surface was greatly speeded and with greater safety as the often considerable elasticity of the rope was removed.

Up until this time the coals were sorted and cleaned below ground in many mines, the dross (dust and stones) being left below ground.

By applying the new methods the collieries were able to respond to the ever increasing demands from industry. Using estimates of the consumption of coal in various industries, Duckham (1970) concluded that the annual coal supply in Scotland had reached around 1.55 million tons by 1800, marking a very substantial increase over the 0.475 million tons produced in 1700.

It was one thing to raise the coals to the surface, but transporting them to the market or consumer was hindered by a poor and often deeply rutted and dangerous road system. In wet weather the horses struggled as the loaded carts sank to their axles in the muddy lanes. Few of the countryside streams were bridged until after the development of turnpike roads began in the mid-eighteenth century. The network of these substantially improved roads did not reach completion until the end of that century. Macadam introduced a formal procedure for construction of the roads using a basis of twenty centimetres of rock aggregate to provide a secure surface. That material, too could become rutted, and he insisted that there should be sufficient material available kept on site to repair holes, often with the help of the local road men, each of whom was responsible for the upkeep of a specific section of roadway. It was not until much later, in 1867, that the surface was bonded together with asphalt, and then only on the major roads. The raising of road quality made considerable improvement in the ability of the miners to carry their produce to the markets or to the dockside.

Two Parliamentary Acts of lasting importance were passed during this period. Although the formality of serfdom, except for miners, had been abolished in England as early as 1399, followed by freeing the miners in 1594, it was not until 1775 that a form of freedom was granted to the Scottish miners. Slavery had been abandoned in Scotland in 1364 but the Act had provisions excluding the collier from this dispensation. This status was reinforced over two centuries later in a further Act of the Scottish Parliament in 1579 in which it was decreed that all females working in the mines should be kept in bondage until the age of eighteen, the males until they were twenty-four years of age. It was not until 1775, that an Act of Parliament effectively proposed to fully free the miners from their bondage. They had hitherto been tied to the mine and whole families were often sold as part of the property. Miners between thirty-five and forty-five years of age were to be freed after serving a further seven years. Even then hurdles were placed in the way of miners wishing to leave the industry or transfer to other mines. For those wishing to join the industry in a formal way, through an apprenticeship, the contract of employment could be hard. Montgomery (1994) quotes the terms, which maintain that the miner 'shall not commit fornication, not contract marriage within the said term for three years' and also 'shall not waste the goods of his said masters, not lend them unlawfully, shall not play at cards or dice, or any unlawful games....shall neither buy nor sell, shall not haunt taverns or playhouses.' All that despite the miners having gained their freedom.

It was not until 1799 that a second Act truly gave freedom of movement without penalty. Even at that time children between nine and thirteen years of age were expected to work below ground for up to twelve hours a day. In 1840 a Parliamentary Commission was set up to examine the conditions under which children were employed in the coal mines. Commissioner Robert Franks found that children as young as six or seven worked below ground, although most began their labours between the ages of eight and nine.

In Eastern Scotland, where conditions were worse than elsewhere in Britain the 2,256 children under thirteen years of age formed an important part of the total workforce of around 9000, and they suffered the same rate of accidents as the adults. One young girl, quoted by Montgomery (1994) recorded that she travelled fourteen fathoms (roughly 27 m) from the work face to the foot of an five metre ladder leading to the mine main road, whence along another road and up three more such ladders to reach the shaft base, where her load of never less than fifty kilograms was placed in a tub. This journey would be completed twenty times each day, along roads usually no more than 1.2m in height. Other harrowing accounts of twelve year-olds working underground for up to ninety-two hours a week, were to follow in the Report. Women miners also endured similar severe working conditions, which are exceptionally well addressed by King (2001), who provides many informative and thought-provoking illustrations. Conditions for all were greatly improved thereafter, with Lord Shaftesbury introducing legislation to ban women and girls, and boys below ten years of age from working underground. The change of labour structure led to a substantial increase in the use of pit ponies, but no evidence has been found of their use in North East Fife.

The development, by George Stephenson in 1841, of a steam locomotive able to move thirty tons of coal on wagons at four miles an hour, opened the way to introducing underground haulage by such means. However, the smoke released caused significant ventilation problems. Placing the engines at the pit head and using long wires or cables to reach to the base of the mine enabled the coals to be lifted readily. Subsidiary steam powered winding machines at depth permitted haulage along the main access routes from remote parts of the mine. The new techniques allowed for the introduction of horizon mining, in which the coal seams could be linked by constructing horizontal access roads driven from the shafts through sturdy coal free rocks. In collieries using this method several coal seams could be worked to the rise simultaneously from a long single main access road or level. If further access roads or levels were driven at higher or lower positions down the shaft they permitted the same coal seams to be worked to the rise from these new horizons using longwall or stoop and room methods as appropriate. An early example of this form of working at Halbeath, Fife, is given by Payne, (1982). (Fig.6)

As in the earliest days of coal mining, gas presented grave dangers to the miners. Some of the gases, such as firedamp were explosive, others produced asphyxia (the stifle). It was suspected that exposure of the gases to the naked candle flames, which were needed to enable the workers to see what they were doing in the otherwise pitch black darkness below ground, was causing many explosions throughout the land. In 1815 Sir Humphry Davy, a chemist who was then President of the Royal Institution in London, was prevailed upon by mine owners in Newcastle to devise a form of safety lamp, which he did with great success, (Galloway, 1882).

A second form of safety lamp was produced at about the same time by George Stephenson. Mercifully most of the Scottish mining areas were relatively, but not totally, free from gas problems, much less so than the mines of north-eastern England and south Wales. These and other hazards, coupled with the depths, often over 300m, at which mining was carried out, led to increasing numbers of accidents and fatalities rose steadily until by 1850 on average 1000 miners were killed in the United Kingdom each year. The first Inspector of Mines, Tremenheere, appointed in 1848 after more than twenty years of demands from the community, faced the problems of an industry with 200,000 workers in 2000 collieries, in which one in every two hundred miners was killed annually. Fortunately for the colliers of North-East Fife, very few local deaths were reported to be directly as a result of such industrial accidents. While the dangers of death by industrial accident were ever present, one of the early medical comments on the physical fitness of the colliers, made by Dr S. Scott-Alison to the Parliamentary Commission of 1842 draws attention to the prevalence of illnesses which could be directly related to the working conditions. He stated that 'between the twentieth and thirtieth year many colliers decline in bodily vigour and become more and more spare; the difficulty in breathing progresses and they find themselves very desirous of some remission of their labour.

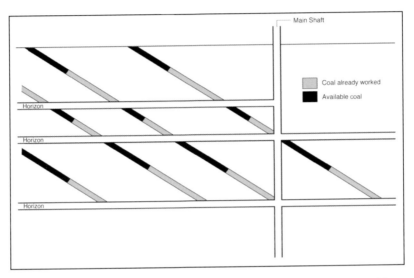

Fig.6. Horizon mining, in which horizontal stone mines are driven to provide access to several coal seams from the one roadway. The coals are worked up the slope of the seam

This period is fruitful in acute diseases, such as fever, inflammation of the lungs and pleura, and many other ailments, the product of over exertion, exposure to cold and wet, violence, insufficient clothing, intemperate and foul air.' His colleague, Dr Thomson, also from Edinburgh, added that workers 'occasionally die of an affection of the lungs accompanied with the expectoration of a large quantity of matter of a deep black colour...'. The life of the collier was a very tough one, commonly shortened by accident or work-induced medical problems.

1850-1913

By 1851, when the total population of Great Britain was 20.8 millions, the miners produced about 58 million tons of coal annually. The country was becoming criss-crossed by networks of steam driven railways, originally developed purely to carry coals to the markets and ports, but increasingly used by passengers to travel from town to town.

A major step in improving ventilation in the mines came with the introduction of compressed air pumps able to move over 5000 cubic metres of air per minute. This also laid the way for compressed air powered cutters to come into service in 1853 for use in longwall workings to replace the need for all coal to be won by manual pick work.

The advent of electricity in 1880 allowed a major advance in the lighting of the main working and access roads. Soon the cutters and pumps were also powered by electricity. Electrically powered winding began in 1900, by which time UK coal production had reached 225 million tons annually, with over 750,000 employed in the industry. The miners were now using carbide or safety lamps in place of candles, but still the annual death toll in UK mines between 1850 and 1910 rose to over a thousand. It was not until 1897 that it was required that mine abandonment plans should be prepared within three months of closure to provide an accurate plan of the mine headings, pillars of coal remaining, position and dip of the seam, depth of shaft, etc. Until that time not infrequently miners unexpectedly encountered former workings, often flooded, with dire consequences. The idea of routinely boring ahead to ascertain conditions and likely hazards was not introduced until later.

With the widespread adoption of mechanised extraction techniques, the era of modern mining had arrived, and the peak of Scottish coal production was recorded in 1913, with 43.2 million tons. With the advance of mining methods had come the production of ever increasing quantities of waste materials which were carried to the surface for disposal in bings. Manual winning of the coals by purely stoop and room or longwall methods involved keeping the wastes almost entirely within the seams themselves. Beyond the material excavated from the shafts, any wastes were from fallen roofs, wall collapse or risen pavements, or from the newly cut access tunnels. Much of this material was left within the abandoned rooms or within the longwall workings with controlled roof collapse. The material released by the mechanised cutters not only produced usable coals but they also generated dust, which was transported to the surface along the conveyors. Any seams with thin internal layers of sandstone were removed completely and the sandstones separated at the surface picking tables operated by women. The peak period for the building of the formerly all too familiar bings was between 1870 and 1920. Fortunately no bings of great size or longevity were formed in the Ceres-St Andrews area, where mining had ceased by 1910, although more substantial remnants of a small bings remain at nearby Radernie.

GEOLOGICAL STRUCTURES

During much of the Carboniferous Period, renewed movements occurred in the earth's crust, principally on the European continent and southern Britain, during the Variscan mountain building episode. The effects of this were felt in Fife, where the successions of coal bearing rocks became deformed into a series of folds, with upwarped arches or anticlines, as on the line between Bandirran and South Callange, and the downwarped basins or synclines, as in the Denhead, (Fig.7) Radernie and Pittenweem collieries. (Fig. 4)

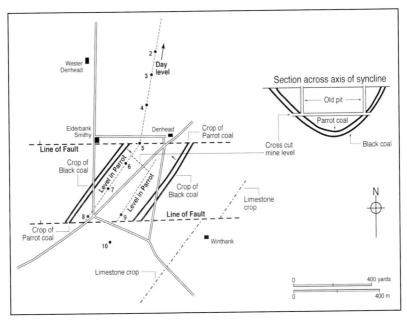

Fig.7. Map of the Denhead syncline showing the outcrops of the Black and Parrot Coals and a cross-section to show the basin-like profile. The dotted line marks the position of the Gowkston day level, and the numbers indicate known sites of the air shafts leading to it. (after McLaren, 1822)

While the anticlines may have been subjected to later erosion and destruction of the coals, the synclines often preserved the coal successions. The deformation was not confined to folding of the rock layers, but also included fracturing, by which the entire successions were split apart along well defined planar surfaces referred to as 'fault planes,' with the rocks on one side raised, or lowered relative to those on the other, as along the Ceres Fault, which trends northeastwards from Ceres to Backfield of Ladeddie where it terminates against the younger Maiden Rock Fault, and the smaller east to west trending faults which truncate the coals of Claremont and Denork in both the northern and southern ends of their outcrops. (Fig.8) Occasionally, the rock masses slid past each other without vertical displacement. Faulting provided problems for the colliers, in that when working below ground they sometimes found the coal seam stopped against a fault. At that stage they needed to decide whether to look for the coal at a higher or lower level on the other side of the fault. Still more problematic was the fact that faults often provide routeways by which waters penetrate into the rocks and an unexpected encounter with a fault could lead to sudden release of this water and flooding of the mine.

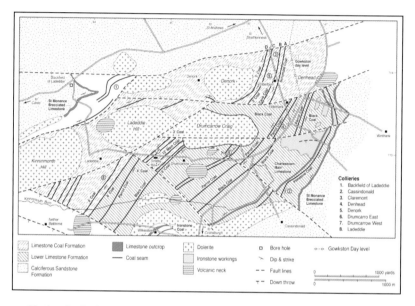

Fig.8. Geological Map of the eastern coalfields, based on information from
Ballingal, Landale Forbes, Pinshon, Gemmel, the British Geological
Survey, and personal observations

Igneous intrusions provide a further geological hazard, as they impinge on the coals to differing extents throughout the district. The igneous rocks were originally of molten materials that were intruded into the pre-existing, often folded and faulted successions of sedimentary rocks. As they cooled from high temperatures (over one thousand degrees centigrade in some cases) they generated crystalline minerals, which formed a very compact texture, making them much harder than the hosting sediments. Two main forms are commonly recognized. Dykes appear as nearly vertical walls of material often three to four metres thick, cutting across the layered rocks. Sills are masses of flat-lying rocks, locally often arranged roughly parallel to the layering of the sedimentary rocks, but may grow to over 30m in thickness in Fife. (Fig.9) Some dykes solidified along fault fracture planes located in the workings immediately east of Ceres.

Typically, many areas of high ground, for example Drumcarrow Craig, Ladeddie and Kinninmonth Hills, are underlain by sills of dolerite, a fine grained crystalline basic rock rich in iron and magnesium minerals. Both sills and dykes were hot when emplaced, and immediately beside their margins the rocks commonly became heated. The sandstones and mudrocks along the margins of the intrusions became hardened, but often the heat passing upwards from the thicker sills burned out the coals encountered, leaving ashes in their place.

In addition to the presence of sills and dykes, a third form of intrusion is also found within north-east Fife, namely volcanic necks. Filled with blocks of lava and broken bed rock surrounded by ash, these masses often form upstanding or prominent points in the landscape. They are present at Drumcarrow, Ladeddie, Denhead, Wilkieston and in two small masses at Callange. From their intrusive nature they break through the layered rocks and sever coal seams. They were injected into the rocks late in the Carboniferous period. Similar volcanic necks are seen at the Rock and Spindle stack on the coast south of St Andrews and the headlands at Elie.

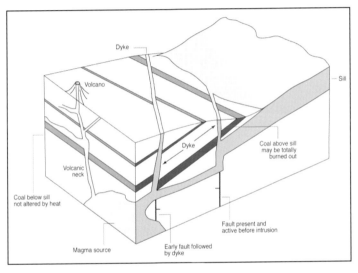

Fig.9. Bodies of igneous rocks arising from a magmatic source.
Sills are parallel to the layering or inclined at low angles.
Dykes are near vertical or steeply inclined, and are often
intruded along pre-existing faults

SUMMARY OF THE STRUCTURE OF THE CERES – ST ANDREWS COALFIELD

The principal coalfields of North-East Fife lie within the boundaries of the parishes of Ceres, Cameron and St Andrews. Their geological characteristics and histories of exploitation as far as is currently known will be addressed as four groups:

1. Ceres, Callange, Kinninmonth
2. Winthank-Cassindonald, Craigton
3. Denork, Claremont, Denhead
4. Drumcarro, Ladeddie, Backfield of Ladeddie

There are almost as many interpretations of the coal basins of the area as geologists who have attempted to elucidate their structure and the identities of the various coal seams. The generally accepted succession of the coals, limestones and intervening sedimentary rocks in East Fife, has been established from the exposed rocks along coastal cliff sections. However, away from the coasts, problems arise from the fact that rocks of the entire area have been subjected to both folding and faulting before and after the intrusion of the many bodies of igneous rock. The latter may overlie or underlie the coal seams, while others line faults, making the interrelationships between adjacent sedimentary sequences difficult to decipher. Furthermore, much of the area has a mantle of glacial tills, unconsolidated pebbly, sandy clays which bury many of the bed rock outcrops. Together these problems mean that individual coals or limestones cannot be traced across the area with certainty.

Landale (1837) provided the first systematic account of the coals, noting also some of the limestones, faults and igneous intrusions in what was the first geological map of most of Fife. The coals of Ceres were shown in a regular succession of layers which was disrupted by a series of north-south trending faults and dykes. At their western extremity, the coals turned towards the north from their normal northeast–southwest pattern of outcrop. Landale believed that this bend was a result of intrusions between the coals and the limestones at Craighall. The dips were steep in the west, but decreased in angle further to the east, so that the outcrop was shown as broadening beyond Callange and Kinninmonth. In a separate group of coals in the Cassindonald to Drumcarro area the succession was shown as generally dipping to the northwest, whereas at Backfield of Ladeddie, in the west, the limestones and coals dipped steeply towards the southeast, indicating the presence of a sharp synclinal fold in this area, which lay between two substantial faults. No coals were shown in the Denork-Denhead area, which was marginal to Landale's survey, the first attempt to map and identify the seams. That he did not identify all of them is not to criticise, because his work provided an important foundation for all those that have followed.

In the first account given by the Geological Survey of Scotland, Geikie (1902), largely repeated the information on the Ceres coalfield from Landale as the workings had ceased 'several generations previously.' Nevertheless he did point out that, despite the presence of faults, the seams were effectively continuous at least as far eastwards as Kinninmonth, but stressed that no direct connection had been established with the seams farther east at

Ladeddie and Drumcarro. He indicated that the latter coals were underlain by the Hurlet Limestone at Backfield of Ladeddie, Winthank and Mount Melville, but again referred to the lack of continuity of the seams as a result of substantial faulting. The presence of an asymmetrical syncline was recognised towards Ladeddie, and a second small symmetrical syncline between Denork and Denhead. Geikie drew attention to the presence of the, by then exhausted, Blackband Ironstones at Winthank and Denhead, pointing out that the ironstone horizons, which lay between two limestones, died out westwards. In his admirable field guide to the Geology of Fife and Angus, MacGregor (1968) noted the presence of many waste mounds associated with the long abandoned Denhead coal workings, and provided a listing of fossils found in the limestones at Backfield of Ladeddie, accepting it as the Hurlet Limestone (i.e. St Monance Brecciated Limestone in local terminology). He did not attempt to enter discussion of the structure of the coalfields themselves.

Following analysis of borehole cores from East Fife, Forsyth and Chisholm (1968) reassessed the basal limestone unit and confirmed that it was the Hurlet Limestone, the equivalent of the St Monance Brecciated Limestone, best seen on the south Fife coast. There it is considered to mark the boundary between the Calciferous Sandstone Measures and the overlying Lower Limestone Formation. The revision of the Geological Survey Memoir by Forsyth and Chisholm (1977) and the associated 1:50,000 scale geological maps in Sheets 41 (Chisholm and others 1970) and 49 (Armstrong and others 1980) maintained this renaming of the limestone at the base of the succession at Ladeddie, Winthank and Mount Melville. They considered the Charlestown Main (Blackhall) Limestone to be the thin limestone above the Blackband Ironstone. The Mid-Kinniny Limestone was also recognised a little higher in the succession. The sharp bend in the layering of the steeply inclined edge coals between Newbigging of Ceres and the eastern end of Ceres village was reinterpreted as lying in a more east-west direction on approach to the Ceres Fault.

The most complete sequence of the rocks of the Lower Limestone Formation followed by the Limestone Coal Formation appears to be present in only one narrow fault-bounded strip of land extending from Cassindonald to Ladeddie.

The names of the principal limestones and coals are listed in Table 1, together with what are believed to be their equivalent names from the west of Fife and west of Scotland areas, where known. The thicknesses of the rock successions between each of the named horizons vary greatly. In some instances the individual seams are no more than a few metres apart, but elsewhere other seams may be separated by over a hundred metres.

COAL OWNERSHIP AND THE WORKING ARRANGEMENTS

At different times, the minerals present beneath the ground have been claimed by the crown or the feudal overlord, normally the estate owner. In the eighteenth and nineteenth centuries the major estates with coal in the south of Fife were worked with the Earl of Kellie and Sir John and Sir Robert Anstruther. In the Ceres-St Andrews district the proprietors included Captain Holmes Rigg of Tarvit (Ladeddie, Drumcarrow and Downfield); Colonel. Thomson, and later Captain Thomson followed by Mr. J.A. Thomson of Charleton (Callange, Ladeddie and Craigton); Sir Thomas Hope, General Hope and Mr. H.W. Hope of Craighall (Callange and Ladeddie); Mr. Durham of Largo (Ladeddie and Claremont); Mr. J.W. Melville (Craigton, Winthank); and Mr. J. Nairn (Denork, Claremont and Craigton). The tithes of the early days later gave way to renting of the lands to the potential exploiters, who paid a lordship either in kind at ten percent of the sales or by means of a fixed annual rent. Since nationalisation of the industry in 1947, the mineral rights are effectively government owned.

In some cases the estate factor or a grieve was given responsibility for running the mines directly on behalf of the owner. More frequently, permission to work the coals was leased to an individual or small company of men either for a short period of exploratory workings or for a longer period once the presence of sufficient coals had been proven. A lease for between twelve and nineteen years was common as it provided time for the lessee to invest in equipment and to make a profit on its working. The lessee was the tacksman, who was given powers to run the operation, usually in consultation with the estate factor. The tacksman would employ a mining oversman who saw to the to day to day problems of the underground workings, while the tacksman or grieve dealt with financial matters such as sales and purchase of equipment, discussing plans for development of the workings, and hiring and firing the workmen and their families. The mining oversman was the manager of operations below ground, allocating colliers to particular work areas, checking that working was as safe as could be achieved, and often playing a role in quality control of the baskets of coals taken 'to the hill' i.e. up the ladders to the surface and deposited on heaps awaiting sale. No customers wished to find they had bought lumps of sandstone or iron pyrites mixed in with their coals.

The miners could operate directly as hewers at the coal face, removing the coals, but they needed the support of other colliers to deal with propping the roof and similar tasks. Drawers or putters, who were usually children of the family, from the age of six dragged the wooden tubs containing half a hundredweight of coal to the foot of the shaft ladder. There they gradually filled large baskets with the coals, which often two men hoisted onto the backs of the women. From the age of fifteen the womenfolk would be expected to carry heavy these loads of the coals 'to the hill'. In the Review of the Coal Trade in Scotland, in 1812, Bald recorded seeing women carrying loads of one and a half hundredweight (77kg) upslope for 150m then up 36m of ladders to the pit head and another 20m to the coal heap. In a ten hour shift they would repeat this feat 24 times for a daily wage of 8d. Other children were employed as trappers in the larger mines to open and close air doors in the workings to provide ventilation. Still more children were employed as pumpers, operating hand pumps in the lowest part of the pit to keep the work rooms dry for excavation. They raised the waters to a level from which the main pumping engine could deal with them. This not unusually involved being waist deep in water for hours on end.

In any single enterprise the numbers of people involved were small, with around a dozen hewers and their support teams. In most workings the hewers operated alone, but at some pits it was found that putting them into pairs and even threes led to substantial increases in production of the coals, as they were able to give each other support when large pieces of coal were being displaced. In 1842 the Drumcarro mine, the largest in the area at that time, employed thirty-eight men nine of whom were between the ages of thirteen and eighteen.

When any major decision about changes to the workings of a particular pit were considered it would have been normal to call in an expert for advice. Such mining engineers were usually attached to a major mine and were hired out to others. These people were most important in weighing up the problems being faced, and often led to fresh coal seams being discovered and exploited. David Landale, who began his career on the Wemyss estate, became one of the most important Mining Engineers in the Fife collieries. In 1835 he was given a major award by the Highland Agricultural Society with whom he published the first geological map of the known coal deposits recognised when travelling round Fife on horseback. Other mining engineers producing reports during the eighteenth and nineteenth centuries included Beaumont, Dixon and Bald, McLaren, Melville and Archibald, Punshon, and Gemmel, but Landale's contributions dwarfed all others in importance, as recognised by the award of an honorary doctorate by the University of St Andrews in 1888.

THE CERES COALFIELD

Many references to coals appear in the Minutes of the Ceres Parish Associate Session, currently held in the University of St Andrews Library, for the period from 1738 onwards. However they usually refer to failure to deliver the coals on time during the winter snows. The most informative early account that we have of the actual mining at Ceres is that of Francis Beaumont. This was written in 1806 after he had interviewed James Edmund and two unnamed but long-serving colliers, said to be the last surviving miners who had worked for Melville and Son, the tacksmen for the site. Usefully, his report of the meeting recorded by Forbes, 1957) included an eye sketch map on which the men identified by name the individual fields along the hill to the south of the B939 Ceres-St Andrews road. No less than seventeen separate coal seams were identified by name, most of which had been worked at some time. In his Report on the Geology of the East Fife Coalfield, Landale (1837) provided a summary of the Ceres coals, (Table 1), based mainly on the findings of Beaumont, noting that although most of the workings had long ceased, 'these coals will some time or other be highly prized and yield a very handsome return.'

In a report on the nearby Callange Coalfield, Landale (1878) referred to the fact that Melville and Sons, by now the third or fourth generation in the business, were working as tacksmen on some of the ground to the west of Callange, but provided no details. Later writings on the coalfield by Geikie (1902) relied principally upon the reports of Beaumont and Landale. No subsequent mining has been carried out although, during the Second World War, the Directorate of Opencast Coal Production carried out trenching around Newbigging of Ceres and borehole exploration west of Callange. They disagreed with Landale to the extent of the viability of reopening any workings at that time. In 1963 an exploratory borehole at Callange by the British Geological Survey penetrated the lower parts of the sequence recorded by Landale (Forsyth and Chisholm, 1977), identifying no less than thirteen of the coal seams.

The Banfield Coal Book, in the reference section of Cupar Library, is an informative week by week account of the financial affairs of a colliery working in the Ceres coalfield between 1749 and 1761. A period of twelve years was not uncommon for the let of a tack or period of renting, to exploit minerals at that time. In his introduction James Melville states that the original contract to work the coals was for fifteen to seventeen years, but it is not clear why the colliery was closed in May 1761. There is no indication that the coals were running out at this time, but water was certainly becoming a problem. Although production of the coals had been somewhat erratic during the preceding year or so, the workings were still showing a substantial profit when last calculated, as indeed they had been through most of the life of the enterprise. The name Banfield has presented a problem in attempting to determine the location of the colliery as it is not marked as such on Beaumont's sketch map of 1806. The outcrop of the lowest, 0.76 cm thick coal seam, is plotted as the Ballfield Coal on the Geological Survey maps of the area. In the preliminary topographic maps produced by Roy in 1746 there is an area towards the crest of the ridge which is marked as Bawfield.or Ba'field.

Ceres	Drumcarro	Largoward/Radernie	West of Fife
Luncart			
Mak-Him-Rich			CardendenLower Smithy
Ceres Two Foot	Three Foot		
Ceres Thick	10 Foot Thick		Seven Foot
Ceres U. Four Foot	Four Foot		Lochgelly Splint
Ceres Six Foot	Eight Foot		Lochgelly Parrot
Little Splint			Pilkin
Bowanton			Glassee
Donaldson			
North			
Ceres Little			Mynheer
Ceres Five Foot	Four Foot		
Ceres L.Four Foot	Six Foot		Five Foot
Ceres Whin			Dunfermline Splint
Ceres Rum			
Johnstone Shell Bed			Shell Bed
Smithy			Smithy
Ceres Black		Largoward Thick	
***************	***********	*************	********************
Upper Kinniny Lst			Top Hosie Limestone
Ballfield			Marl Coal
Mid-Kinniny Lst			Second Hosie Lst
Lower Kinniny Lst			Mid Hosie Lst
Coal	Parrot	Largoward Parrot & Splint	
Coal	Black	Largoward Black	
Charlestonwn Main Lst			Blackhall Lst
Coal	Cannel	Radernie Marl	
Coal	Rums	Radernie Maain	
Coal	Ironstone Splint	Radernie Duffie	
St Monance Little Lst			Inchinnan Lst
Coal	Low Little	Radernie Brassie	
St.Monance Brecciated Lst			Hurlet Limestone

Table 1. The succession of the principal coals and limestones in the Ceres area and their possible equivalents at Drumcarro and Largoward and also in the west of Fife, partly from Forsyth and Chisholm (1977).

The site may have been that of an early recreation area, possibly a football field, on the flatter ground above the sloping hill face. It is a small step to envisage the name becoming further transliterated to or from Banfield. An undated map quoted by M.martin in his excellent detailed web accounts of pits in Fife shows 'Ballfield Cottages' north of the Ceres to Baldinnie Road, south of Coaltown of Callange.

On a plan of the day level of the Callange mine, workings produced by Melville on behalf of the Collier Club and presented to John Thomson, and dated 6th November 1754, the lowest coal seam has the label Ballfield Coal on the eastern side of a prominent fault, but the same seam is clearly referred to as the Banfield Coal on the western side of the fault. Both titles seem to have been in use in the mid-eighteenth Century. To avoid confusion in this account the coal seam will be referred to here as the Ballfield Coal and the colliery as the Banfield colliery.

According to Beaumont (1806), the Ballfield Coal and the overlying Black Coal, the lowest two seams, are separated from the main group of the Ceres Coals by 64 metres of barren sediments, and a further 91metres are present between the two seams. The Ballfield Coal was worked below Colonel Thomson's lands of Ballochton, but it was not known to have been accessed in the grounds of Callange where it is certainly present. Melville's record of a new shaft at Banfield, 'entered upon on 8th December, 1749' shows that the shafters were to be paid at a rate of '£3 per fathom to ye limestone and £6 per fathom to ye pavement'. The position of the Ballfield Coal beneath a limestone suggests that it should be equated with the Marl Coal of Largoward, which is recorded as being discontinuous elsewhere in Fife. It is notably present in a borehole at Lathallan, six kilometres to the southeast, where the limestone is considered to be the equivalent of the Upper Kinniny Limestone. So the Ballfield Coal is the uppermost coal seam of what is properly known as the Lower Limestone Formation. This provides independent support for the suggested position of the coal given in the account of the area by Forsyth and Chisholm, (1977).

The succession of the seventeen coal seams was discovered initially as a result of employing men to dig trenches through the cover of glacial deposits. In the accounts book this activity was variously known as 'break of ground' or 'ground break', for which the diggers were rewarded with ten shillings per week. This may well be the origin of the term ground-breaking applied to apparent advances in knowledge today. In the Ceres area (Table 1), most of the seams located were of adequate thickness to be suitable for some exploitation in the early days of mining. All were inclined northwards at a slightly steeper angle than the slope of the hillside. (Fig 10)

Although initially they may all have been worked at their outcrops on the land surface, the records show that in addition to the Ballfield Coal, itself high on the hillside, seven of the overlying seams were worked at the Banfield colliery, namely the Thick, Four Foot, Six Foot, Little Splint, the Lower Five Foot, Lower Four Foot, and the Whin Coals. The first four of these, the uppermost coals, are only 19.5m apart, and were taken from workings low on the hillside, near to the present Ceres to Callange footpath, formerly known as the Coal Road, which runs east from School Hill Road. Although the coal seams worked are the same at Ceres and Callange, quite different sets of extraction problems were encountered. Firstly the coals worked mainly from the White Den, from the Ballfield to the North Coals will be considered.

The oldest and lowest of the White Den Coals is the Ballfield Coal, approximately 100m below the Black Coal. It outcrops along the crest of the hill and in the Banfield Colliery was principally accessed from a series of vertical shafts high up the hillside, where the seams dip at low angles to the west. From the Ballfield seam Melville carried air vents to the surface, emerging on the common lands. As indicated above, the records of the shafters confirmed that the coal itself lay directly beneath the Limestone. Banfield Colliery lay to the east of the White Den march wall and extended beyond the wood which presently straddles the Ceres-Callange footpath. An engine house had been erected above the pits, but in 1806 the colliers indicated that they had no knowledge of it having been used in their time (i.e. since the 1770s). Its position suggests that it may have been used to

service early workings on the Ballfield Coal. There is no reference in any reports seen to indicate that the Black Coal was ever exploited here.

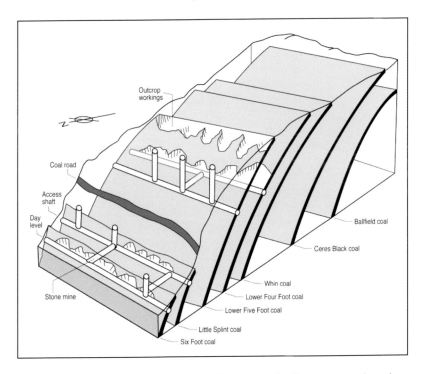

Fig.10. The coal seams of the Ceres White Den gradually steepen northwards.
Both surface outcrop working and extraction from day level tunnels were
normal here, with access shafts arranged above the level tunnels.
The position of Coal Road is indicated

Above the Ballfield and Black coals, the upper seams referred to as the White Den Coals are only 26m apart. With the exception of the Whin Coal, where the groundwater was very close to the seam, the coals were worked to the rise from levels draining westwards into the White Den gulley. The accounts book tells us that cross-cut mines were constructed from the coals at the base of several of the service shafts at Banfield. Because the coal seams were closely spaced, only relatively short horizontal tunnels or stone mines were needed to connect two or three neighbouring seams. This form of development reduced the numbers of shafts needed to extract the coals, and was therefore of considerable economic benefit to the tacksmen. Beaumont showed that the Little, Lower Ceres Five Foot, Lower Ceres Four Foot and Whin Coals lay within 26m of each other. The main group of the White Den Coals were extracted from shafts situated a little above and south of the Coal Road. The unwanted excavated rock material from the cross-cut tunnels was retained in rooms from which the coals had previously been removed. There is no sign of the wastes above ground. The accounts book indicates that as the workings progressed problems arose with the ground waters, thus most of the White Den Coals which outcropped above and south of the Coal Road were worked from a series of levels and shafts.

Melville's accounts book shows that, throughout the life of the Banfield operations, fresh access and air shafts around 50m deep were cut to the working levels in the coals every nine months or so. A linear succession of shafts of similar depth was developed as the workings progressed beneath the hillside. These shafts were arranged along the path of the working level. Each shaft took between eight and fifteen weeks to complete. Although some of the hewers were involved in the sinkings, there were specialists who were employed only for the shafting. The shafters may have worked for other enterprises or elsewhere on the estate when not at Banfield. In the early stages of working the pits the hewers operated independently, but as time progressed, they were paired up which greatly increased their productivity, and there were still further increases when three or even four were encouraged to work together.

In February 1756 a shaft put down to the Thick Coal at a position close to the western boundary of the Banfield grounds penetrated 9.5m below the day level. In addition to the Thick Coal, the Five Foot Coal and the Four Foot Coals were both worked by cross-cut mines, and drained to a sump below the day level. The White Den coals were worked down to the levels where the ground waters became problematic.

In a second series of workings lower down the hillside, shafts were put down to the upper part of the White Den Coals, referred to as the Thick, the Five Foot, Four Foot and Whin Coals. These were separated by a total of only 20m of sandstones and shales. The accounts book shows that Melville worked three of the seams by cross-cut mines from shafts linked to a second drainage level, situated downslope from the Coal Road. The westernmost shaft on this new level met waters 7.3m below the surface, and these waters were pumped and released into the gulley as the full set of seven seams, which lay within 20m of each other, were again made accessible for working.

Many of the shafts to the east of the gulley are known to have penetrated between 44m and 53m from the surface, even in the steeply inclined seams. The Thick Coal, the uppermost of the White Den Coals, contained two distinct layers, the upper part of which was of poor quality and was normally left in place to act as a roof for the lower part, a good quality splint coal. Individual coal seams are notorious for varying in their thickness from location to location, and virtually all of the seams became reduced in thickness towards the west. Occasionally, reference is made to hewers working in their rooms in this coal, which implies that it was exploited by room and stoop rather than by longwall working.

Beneath the upper part of the hill, this group of coal seams was gently inclined towards the north as confirmed by the deeply pitted and tree-covered surface of the wooded area. This site probably marks the location of former shallow room and stoop workings in the gently inclined seams, where roof collapse has now taken place. On the lower ground the seams are recorded as sharply steepening to become almost vertical edge coals about the level of the Coal Road track, as shown on the Geological Survey map, which indicates the presence of former exposures with the rocks inclined at 87 degrees below the White Den gulley. According to various geological and sketch maps, the outcrops of the coal seams begin to turn to the north near the line of the White Den gulley itself, where a strong north-south oriented fault crosses the Coal Road at the junction with the track to Newbigging of Ceres farm.

The present Coal Road footpath, leading past the houses at the east end of School Hill Road, was the principal routeway leading from Ceres through the pits towards Callange. Immediately uphill, to the south of this footpath, is Potters Bank; beyond this is the White Den field area whose eastern limit is marked by the bush-lined gulley. This routeway of the waters discharged from the Banfield day levels, which drained the coal seams present beneath the hill, effectively defined the greatest depth from which the coals were taken in any one level. A geological fault trending nearly parallel to the line of the gulley served to displace the coal seams upward on its western flank, severely reducing the amount of coal between the fracture plane and Ceres village. No record has been found to confirm whether any of the coals beneath the White Den and Potters Bank fields west of the White Den gulley were worked beneath the hill, but they were worked in the low area immediately east of the village. The only indication of any early workings in this area seen today is in the brightly coloured ochrous waters which emerge into gardens of houses to the west of the Ceres-Baldinnie road at the edge of Ceres village. These are said to be drainage waters from the Craighall colliery, to the south of the village, and outside the area currently under consideration.

Despite the reported degeneration of the coals, in the flat land to the west of Bess Watts Bank is marked the location of a fire engine at a pit some 45m deep, so the coals were actually worked in that area prior to abandonment in 1761. The plan marks the position of the formerly worked coal some way north of the engine pit location, suggesting that the coals may have again taken on a less steep inclination. The fire engine certainly pumped waters up to the ditch from the day levels described above. Unfortunately no references to the actual workings at this particular site have been located beyond a note on the 1806 map stating that the lowest level was worked in rooms. It is possible that the coal workings from shafts near the Coal Road may have linked up with this area of working as they would have been at very similar levels below the ground. We do not know for certain. Again the coal seams were believed to be undisturbed north of this line.

To the north and downhill from Coal Road track, and to the east of the day level ditch lies Bess Watts Bank, beneath the southern 200-300 metres of which, Beaumont was told, the Callange Coals had been removed and the workings then filled with wastes.

Farther north, beneath the Bess Watts Bank area, the coals were still believed to be present and undisturbed. No evidence was given to support this assertion, but the sketch map shows, a little below the track, the site of a disused pit which was said to have been formerly worked with the aid of a horse driven winding wheel. There is also an indication of the site of an old outcrop working in the south-eastern corner of the Bank.

Within the wooded area to the south of the Coal Road, the ground is characterised by a concentration of hollows which appear to mark either the collapsed roofs of near surface drift mines or the tops of a cluster of adjacent pit shafts. This ground must be regarded as potentially unstable and should be entered only with great caution.

In general, the Ceres coals were considered to be of good quality Cherry coals, which burned with a bright cheerful flame, but in the northwestern part of the field the coal quality decreased sharply, into what is commonly referred to as 'foul' coal. The degeneration of the coals towards the foot of the hill may be in part due to the known presence of several bodies of intrusive igneous rocks, from which gases and fluids would have penetrated the rocks and chemically attacked the coals during and soon after their emplacement. The dykes of igneous rock and several faults (hitches) also served to sub-divide the areas or panels of workable coals. Across the higher part of the coalfield the rocks are inclined towards the north or northwest at dips of one in three or one in four from the horizontal, somewhat steeper than the slope of the land surface. However, as indicated above, the White Den rock succession steepened towards the Coal Road to become near vertical edge coals. The upper coal seams, which outcrop to the north, are believed to have continued in this steep orientation into the lands immediately east of the village.

In the Bess Watts Bank area, the Thick, Four Foot, Six Foot, Little Splint and Bowanton seams of the Ceres Coals were worked between two of the substantial dykes of igneous rock, the eastern one of which lay within the Ballochton grounds. The whole of this colliery was said to have been 'in a very trumbled state,' implying the presence of very irregular early workings. Several tacksmen were said to have worked there over the years, each exploiting the coals for short term gain, abandoning the site when problems arose. The 'ruined' colliery was in a dangerous state and Beaumont advised against any attempt to resurrect the property. He did, however, suggest that some exploration in the Ballochton grounds to the east might be worthwhile, although its limited area suggested that reserves would be small. It should be noted that the British Geological Survey maps show that the Ceres Fault, one of the major fault lines of Fife, along which the rocks to the south are estimated to have been downthrown by over 100m, is thought to be located beneath or towards the north of Bess Watts Bank. In a locality so close to the major fracture the presence of many small faults might be expected to occur, so the apparent poor condition of the mine may not have been entirely the result of poor mining practice, but partly due to the many geological problems encountered.

More attention will be given to the Callange Coals and their structural problems in the next section.

The quantities of coal extracted are quoted in loads, and in Fife a load approximated twenty-two stones Dutch. (The Dutch stone weighed sixteen pounds, so a load was between one and two hundred kilograms). At most it was about 50% more than the heaviest weight carried to the surface by each bearer each time she climbed the shaft ladders. Six loads would have made a very good cart burden for the market. From the production figures of between one to two hundred loads per week for about nine months, it is evident that relatively few hewers actually worked the mines at any one time. The annual production from the Banfield workings varied between 829 tons and 2720 tons. In its twelve year life the mine showed a total profit of £7830, having run at a loss between 1753 and 1755. The annual rent paid to the estate was £300.

Hewers		Shafters
David Armit		Jo Duff
Tom Aitken		James Fayel
Robert Anderson		Iain Greig
James Cally		Thomas Lawson
Robert Duff		James Melville
Thomas Duff		Davis Miles
Robert Melville		David Miller
David Morrice		James Tyels
Alex Pearson		Robert Wemyss
Martin Rae		
Jo Robeson		
James Roger		
Norman Wemyss		

Table 2. Names of colliers recorded in the Banfield Book.

The Banfield Book also lists the numbers of coal loads produced by individual and groups of hewers. From these one can find the names of both the hewers and also of the shafters. The number of people employed directly in the colliery during the twelve years was not great, a total of thirteen hewers and nine shafters. No less than nine of the hewers were at times redeployed to assist with the shafting, and three of the listed hewers appeared on the record sheets on one single occasion. Supporting the hewers would have been perhaps a further twenty family members. A list of the identified hewers and shafters (Table 2) reveals many names which remain familiar in the area today. No reference was made to James Edmund, to whom Beaumont (1806) attributed much of his knowledge of the area. For most of the period of working, the wages of the hewers were paid by the estate, by whom they were owned. However, for short periods the book shows that these wages were actually paid by the tacksman, at around one pound per man per week. The accounts book also shows that the individual hewer was not confined to working in a single seam, but was moved from seam to seam. Between the summers of 1755 and 1760, the weekly output of coal was normally about 300 loads, reaching over 500 loads on several occasions. During the winter of 1760-61 the weekly production fell to between 29 and 91 loads in four consecutive winter months, but recovered to over 300 loads in March and April before the colliery suddenly closed in May, apparently without warning. It is presumed that the areas of dry and drained coals had been largely mined out by then.

Why did the Banfield colliery at Ceres fail? There is no indication that the coals had been worked out, but it is recognised that extraction from saturated steeply inclined coal seams is far from easy. The early construction of several day levels from the White Den gave clear indication of the presence of water within the rocks of the hill, and provided drainage for the upper zones of the coalfield. The financial accounts in the Banfield Coal Book reflect the need to employ firstly one and later two people to hand pump waters to allow access to the coals. The first mention of water becoming a problem was in February of 1756 when a shaft put down to the westernmost part of the Thick Coal was continued some 8.8m below the day level. The installation of scaffolding enabled two additional rooms to be worked in the steeply inclined seam. Below the scaffolded section the sump held the drainage waters for about six hours. At first this water was pumped out by one man 'in an hour or two.' However, the weekly costs of pumping rose steadily as the water inflow increased, rising from £1/14/- on 27th March to £4/4/- by mid-May and to £11/14/- by 19th June, when a note was added 'This week ye Thick Coal was given up as two pumps were not able to keep down the water occasioned by a lather in the pavement.'

In the flat land at the foot of the hill a fire engine pumped the waters from a worked level in two stages up the 40m deep shaft and discharged them into the drain. We have no knowledge of which coals were being worked at that site, but they were most probably some of the upper coals in the list given in Table 1. Beaumont suggests that the coals to the north of this level remained untouched although probably water saturated. The projected line marking the northern margin of coal workings lies a little south of the B939 road between Ceres and St Andrews. It also appears to lie north of the path of the Ceres fault as shown on existing geological maps of the area, so the prospect of substantial further deposits being accessible today in this area is not great.

To the east of Ceres village and south of Newbigging of Ceres, above the old Coal Road a series of exploratory trenches were put down in 1943 by the Directorate of Opencast Coal Production, (Forsyth and Chisholm, 1977). These revealed that the total thickness of the coal-bearing succession of rocks was much less than that quoted by Landale in 1837. Between the Little Splint Coal, ten metres below the widely worked Six Foot Coal and the base of the Whin Coal, the thickness was 47m compared with Landale's 68m estimate. No further exploration for potential reserves of coal in this area has since been undertaken.

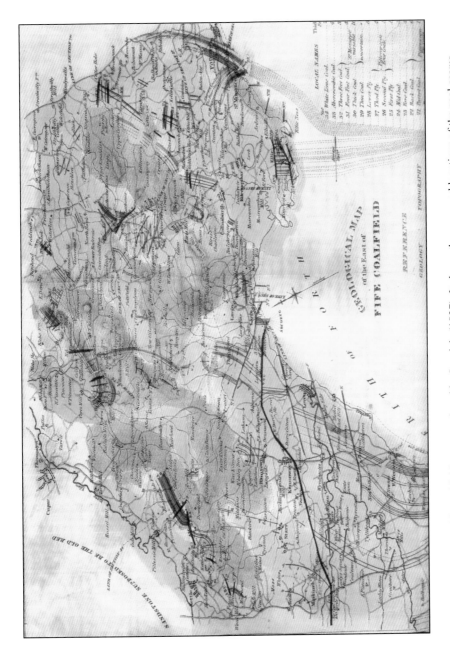

Part of the first Fife coalfield map, produced by Landale (1837). It shows the supposed locations of the coal seams, limestones, faults and igneous intrusions. Black lines are coal, green lines limestone, blue areas dolorite

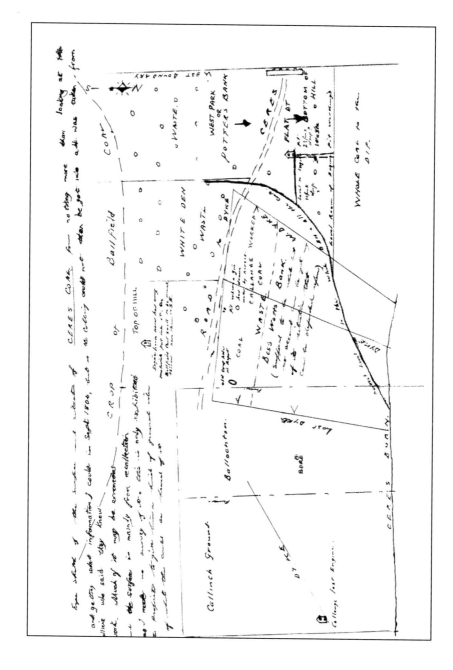

The 'eye-sketch' of the Ceres Coalfield as produced by Beaumont in 1806, following discussions with the last three miners to have worked in the Ceres coals. NB North is towards the base of the map

44

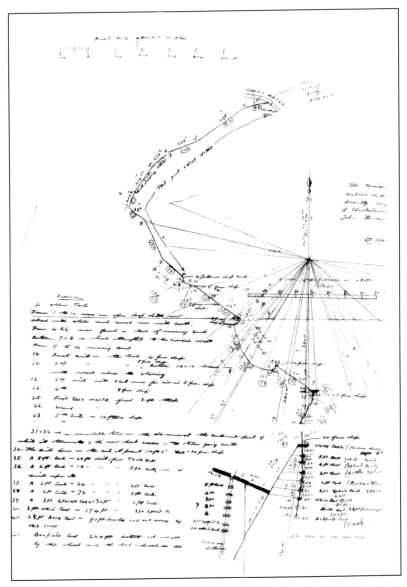

Part of the 1754 plan of the Callange day level tunnel, which led waters into the
Kinninmonth Burn (here referred to as the Ceres Water) at Marley's Hole. In
The base of the plots coal numbered 42 is referred to as the Banfield and
Ballfield Coal on opposite sides of the fault

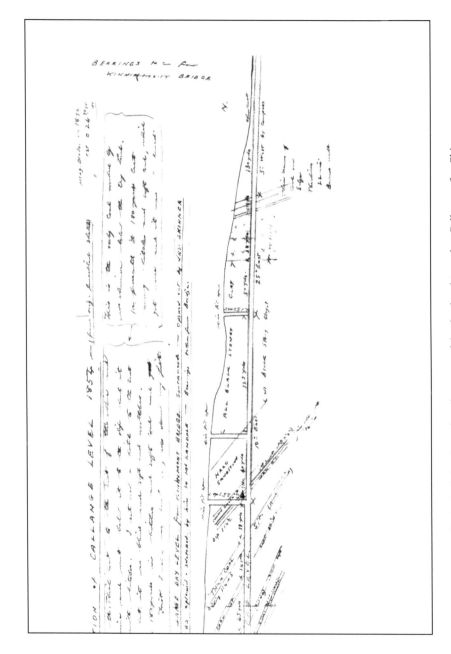

Geological sketch section along part of the day level tunnel at Callange after Skinner (1854) had refurbished the structure from the Kinninmonth Bridge in the north

Orange water flowing from the Callange day level
into the Kinninmonth Burn at Marley's Hole

Collapsed top of bell pit shaft at Drumcarrow Livery Stables

Top of No.8 access shaft, Denhead Coalfield, Drumcarrow Livery Stables

Top of infilled access shaft at Greigston Farm

Access shafts in field along the seam working line direction, Greigston Farm

Outcrop of hard and soft bands including coal
east of Backfield of Ladeddie farm

Coalfield immediately south of Newbigging of Ceres

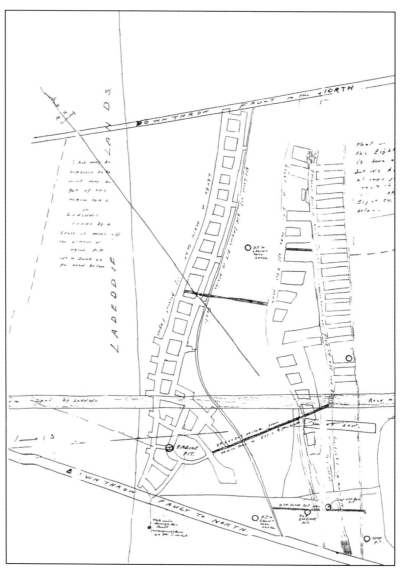

Copy of an undated plan of the western Drumcarro coalfield made by Forbes
From an original plan in the National Coal Board Offices at Wemyss. It
shows two service levels and worked rooms in both the Main Coal
and the Five Foot Coal, the positions of the cross-cut mines
and the location of various pits

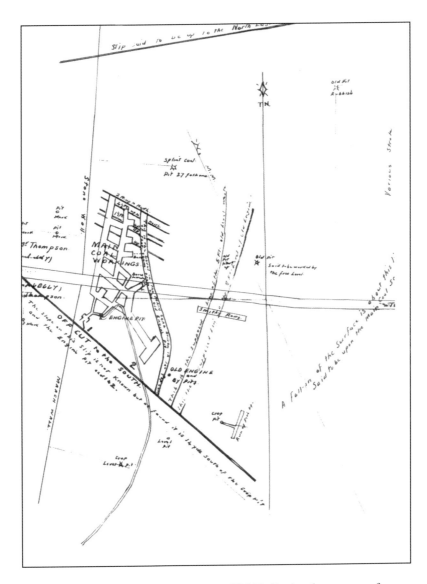

Undated map of the Drumcarro coalfield indicating the presence of
shaft tops in the Ladeddie estate grounds

Central mound is cover of 450 ft deep shaft, Wester Drumcarrow

A sample of the dunstane from the top of the Blackband Ironstone at Winthank

That the Callange coals were worked for a long time is beyond dispute. The present farm of North Callange, a centre of mining in the eighteenth and nineteenth centuries, lies two kilometres east of Ceres, on the B940 road from Pitscottie to Peat Inn. It is not clear when the mining activity began or finally ceased at Callange. According to Dixon and Ball (1808), in a report for General Hope of Craighall, the tacksman Andrew Watt gave up working the coals at North Callange and also at Kinninmonth in 1700, due to a shortage of finance. The mining recommenced at a later date because there are plans, dated 1751 and 1754, dedicated by Mr William Melville, a tacksman to Mr John Thomson of Charleton, showing the workings and detail of the newly completed day level. The principal tacksmen of the eighteenth century were Melville and Sons, the same company that also worked the White Den coals to the west. In his 1837 account of the Geology of the East Fife Coalfield, Landale made only passing reference to coals having been worked at Callange. However, in 1878 when the Callange Coal Company, led by Mr. Nicol, was seeking to terminate its operations on the property, Landale prepared a fuller assessment of the coals for Mr Henry Walter Hope of Luffness, the then estate owner. He obtained a statement from a different Andrew Watt, coal grieve at Dysart, to the effect that the workings at Kinninmonth and Callange had been abandoned by 1862 for lack of money after only two years had elapsed of a nineteen year lease originally from Colonel Hope of Craighall. According to Melville and Sons the succession of coal seams was very similar to that quoted at Ceres by Beaumont, although the thickness of the individual seams often differed

coal seam	thickness (m)
Sparkie	0.6
Lunkart	1.4
Mak-him rich	1.1
Two Foot	0.6
Thick	4.0
Four Foot	1.2
Two Foot (Six ft Beaumont)	0.6
Little Splint	0.8
Bowandon (Rum/blind)	0.8
Donaldsons	0.5
North Coal	0.9
Splint	0.8
Two Foot	1.5
Splint	1.1
Whin Coal	1.0
Black Coal	0.8
Ballfield	0.9

Table 3. The succession of coals at Callange. Estimates
by Melville (1751) and Beaumont (1806).

With the exception of the uppermost three coals, the Sparkie, Lunkart and Mak-him-rich, all of the seams identified by Beaumont (1806) were recognised as extending eastward from the Ceres grounds into the lands of Callange. According to Andrew Watt, of the thirteen seams recorded, the nine which were good enough were originally worked from level roads leading at right angles from the main north to south trending day level. (Fig.11) Later, steam engines were erected north and west of North Callange Farm steading where a pit was put down 62m, and a deeper drainage level constructed 21m beneath the main day level. With the aid of a steam engine this was used to drain as far as the Whin Coal, providing access to considerable reserves at this lower position.(Fig 12)

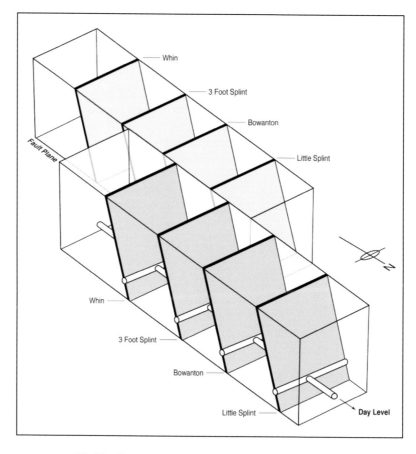

Fig.11. Three dimensional representation of the form of
workings at Callange in the early eighteenth century

The Black and Ballfield Coals were not accessed from this lower level. No coals were extracted from below the Engine Pit level, and they are believed to remain untouched at deeper levels. From the mid-eighteenth century, the Callange mines were drained by day-levels, at least one windmill, and later by steam engines. The most striking feature of the workings is the substantial almost centrally placed main day level which drained most of the seams in the field.. The level, which gradually falls in height towards the north, has its exit at Marley's Hole which lies at 63m above Ordnance Datum on the west side of the Ceres Water, (now the Kinninmonth Burn) a metre or so upstream of the present Callange road bridge. In the north the original day level, for which there exist several plans dated in the 1750s, and a later survey by James Skinner, dated 1852-3 initially took the form of an open ditch along a line bearing south-west for about 200m. The open ditch turned sharply south-east for 100m before being carried below the rising ground surface. After another 250m, the tunnel passed below the eastern side of the North Callange Farm steading before turning to a line south by west. After 50m, it encountered the northward dipping Thick Coal and thereafter continued on the same line, cutting through the entire coal succession until, just over one kilometre from Marley's Hole, it reached the 0.74m thick Black Coal at a depth of 45m below the surface. A Fire Engine shown on a map of 1775 was located on the day level some 57m north of the contact with the Black Coal. In the early 1860s, Watt confirmed the succession of the coals. He also explained that the Black Coal had been worked from and drained by a level branching eastward from the day level and serviced by a windmill. The day level into the Callange coals was carried no further than the Black Coal, but had it proceeded it would have cut the Ballfield Coal seam after a distance of 91m. This is the last known seam to the south. Had the level been continued into the Ballfield Coal it was estimated that it would have drained to a position six or seven rooms, ten to twelve metres below the workings drained by an earlier level in Colonel Thomson's land of Ballochton, known to have been at a depth of 55m. All of the seams except the Bowanton or Rum Coal were of good quality.

A significant north-east to south-west trending fault was crossed by the day level tunnel close to the Thick Coal, with the rocks to the northwest downthrown. The divergence of directions between the day level tunnel and the fault line meant that the more the working progressed to the south the greater the breadth of workable coals that became available. Skinner (1854) noted that the dips of the coals decreased as the fault was approached from the east, making the working easier. The plan dated 1754 shows that to the west of the fault the coals were also worked from a shallow draining level in a north-south trending cross-cut mine rising southwards to 5.5metres below the surface level. Accessed from the Thick Coal where it was serviced by three shafts the level began 45m west of the fault and gradually converged upon it, but not intersecting it before reaching the Whin Coal. There is no known written record of these workings to the west of the fault, where the area available for coal extraction within the Callange ground east of the Ballochton March dyke was limited.

The fire engine referred to on the 1775 map was one of the earliest used in the northeast of Fife. It attracted much interest and wariness lest jobs might be lost for drivers of the horse gins. Indeed the Minutes of the Ceres Associate Parish Church Session of 13th August 1777 reveal an enquiry into damage sustained by the pump head into which holes had been drilled, apparently during visits by a number of men one evening the previous month. Although none admitted knowledge of how the damage had come about, six men, John Griffeth, William Lamb, John McNiesh, Robert Spears, Alex Watson and James Watson were rebuked by the Session for entering the pit without permission, as were David Gourlay, John Hodge, John Sandyman and David Wood for assisting their going down. At that time capital punishment was the penalty for damaging mine machinery.

In the absence of a plan of the workings to the east of the fault, Skinner (1854) reported that the coals were known to have been taken initially for a distance of at least 55m each way from the bases of a series of service shafts along the line of the day level. Each of the seams was worked eastwards along the strike direction (horizontal in the coal seams) and to the rise. The eastward heading of the levels within the coal seams led into old waste-filled workings, at least one of which was cleared out to create an escape pit some 46m deep. The Thick Coal appears to have been exhaustively worked as the seam was much less steeply inclined here, dipping to the north at one in five in the eastern levels.

On the 1751 version of the plan, pit shafts are shown at irregular spacings along the line of the day level, each marking the intersection of the day level with one of the coal seams. These were shafts by which the coals were taken to the surface. In Skinner's section from 1854 three pits are shown to the north of the Thick Coal and a further two within 120m on the Black Coal. The northern of these two crossed two blind coals above the day level but did not actually penetrate to the Black Coal.

Skinner appended a note to a copy of his survey sent to Landale to the effect that he had worked the Thick Coal to the dip, ie. downwards, east of the day level but soon encountered faults and despite persevering for a further 165m, found nothing but soft or blind coals before abandoning the working. It is probable that he had worked into the proximity of a fracture zone associated with the major east-northeast to west-southwest trending Ceres Fault which is believed to be present somewhere in that area,

No coals were extracted from below the level of a second Engine Pit, located west of the North Callange steading, and they are believed to remain untouched at deeper levels. However, about 30m west from the bottom of the Engine Pit, the Thick Coal is known to have been cut into by a rugged whinstone rock, which the Geological Survey staff believed to be a small volcanic neck. Excavation in that direction was ended. Boreholes by Cochrane put down 400m to the west of North Callange Farm identified two coals at 15 and 26m below the land surface. These two coals are probably the Luncart and Mak-Him-Rich coals which are known to lie above the Ceres Thick Coal. They are thought to have been possibly changed by proximity to the volcanic material or the Great Dyke referred to as being near the March wall between the Callange grounds and those of Miss Bess Watts. The entire coal succession was worked eastwards for 300m from the line of the Engine Pit level, until the seams were cut off along a dyke and the substantial fault.

Once installed the engine was heavily used and was kept at work throughout the winter season for six or eight months together without stopping to clean out the boiler. In summer, about eight or nine hours a day were sufficient for the engine to remove the water. Thus the Callange coals were worked from two different levels, the upper day level, and the lower level pumped by the engine. (Fig.12)

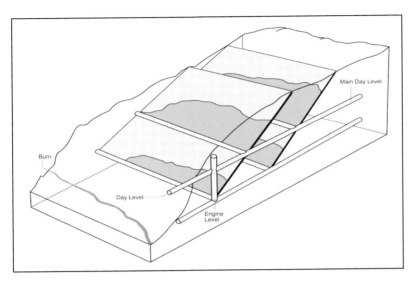

Fig.12. The two levels of working the Callange Coals in 1775

In 1860 Watt put down three pits in the area east of North Callange Farm. The deepest of these was 30m, at which depth he located a seam of coal 1.2-1.4m thick, with a stone layer in the middle of it 5-8cm thick. He worked it for no more than ten weeks before encountering a fault 'which lay from dip to crop', and yielded a considerable quantity of water, but, as he had no machinery to drain it, the working was abandoned.

Watt also put down several boreholes to the north, to depths of 22m and found that the rock layers dipped regularly, but lacked coals. Later he went eastwards to the Dam Park where he bored to the depth of 13m but each of the holes discharged large volumes of water. When Landale examined the borings that had been made farther south in the Cow Park, a field east of the steading, he found the layers very irregularly arranged and declared that 'there appears no great prospect of much coal being found here'. To the south and east of these bores lay the wastes made by Watt on the Four Foot coal (which here, somewhat confusingly, was five feet thick) which had been worked by a day level mine. The outcrop of this coal was traced for about 440m eastwards, but as no bores had been put down to the dip the full extent of this coal remains unknown.

According to his lease from General Hope, Watt was to pay one tenth of the gross output of the coals per annum of rent, but he never paid any. He had no funds to enable him to persevere with the work but, in his opinion, he would have succeeded if he had been able to go on with the colliery. This assertion was supported by the declarations of colliers James Arnot and William Sart.

In 1877, the workings, now a short distance below Coaltoun of Callange, encountered a borehole which leaked very large quantities of water and drowned out the operations for four months. At that time they had to purchase and bring coal to the workings to keep the engines working to get the water out, Once the borehole was properly plugged the water was again manageable and the winning of coals resumed.

In 1878, Landale visited the colliery of the Callange Coal Company to report on how far the tacksmen had fulfilled the conditions and stipulations in the missive of let, and whether they should be allowed to fill up the pits and abandon the colliery. He noted that they would be required to make some record of what had been found and exploited, to be of use to any future tenants who might wish to make some connection with the seams of the White Den. He believed that further work could be carried out in that regard, 'although not in these times and with such people as the Callange Coal Company, every one of them being entirely ignorant of the business.' He was clearly not impressed by the quality or skills of either the workforce or management.

Landale noted that there were several filled or partly filled pits in the north of the Callange grounds, and that although trial pits had been put down, any coals found had been worked only for short periods before being abandoned. Boreholes frequently encountered wastes filling old and unrecorded workings.   Nevertheless the Callange Coal Company had found and worked two seams the upper one 0.74m and the lower 0.84m thick, lay below it. On these they sank a pit and once again worked it for a few months, the upper coal being of poor quality and costly to work so they 'did little with it.' A second pit was sunk 73m deep to the second coal which was of coarse, rough coal, with a good deal of pyrites which made it sulphurous to burn and produced a lot of grey ash. This coal sold at the pit at six shillings per ton for steam coal, but the dross 'could not be sold at any price'.

This coal was expensive to work on account of its bad roof which meant that it had to be excavated entirely within the thickness of the seam. The Company originally paid three shillings per ton for the labour alone, but when this was reduced to two shillings and nine pence, they experienced difficulty in finding men prepared to work at this price, and only six remained in the pit. The workings which continued used longwall methods with the access roads cut in grey sandstone and 0.45m of the weaker mudstone or shale. This was a relatively dry seam, and the winding was powered by a small engine steamed by two boilers.

Some fifteen colliers were normally employed by the Callange Coal Company and the demand for coal was never fully met. The greatest number of colliers working in winter was twenty, and their day's work of 1.25 tons each was never exceeded. Shaw, who worked in Colonel Thomson's lands until 1871, indicated that at that time the coals sold for one shilling and three pence per load of twenty Dutch stones. Watt believed that the normal demand would have steadily employed twenty colliers. Most of the dross produced was consumed by the engines.

The accounts books of 1877reveal that 3169 tons of coal and 40 tons of dross had been sold from the operations at between six shillings and six and seven pence a ton, which, at a royalty of nine pence per ton should have generated £118:16:9d for the estate. The Company estimated that exploration and fittings had cost about £6000 and wages around £3000. Much of the overall loss was attributed to the drowning out of the workings. Landale agreed that closure of these northern workings should be permitted to go ahead.

Before reaching the stage of seeking to close the workings a number of exploratory boreholes had been put down, mainly to the north and west of Callange Farm, but two at Kinninmonth were also recorded. The borers were Claude Thomson, of Harthill and Cochrane of Lochgelly, both reputable in their field. Examples of the logs of the borings as recorded by Landale (1878) are given in Appendix 1. They revealed the presence of two thin coal seams and one 1.35m thick at a depth of 26m at Kinninmonth. The coals were thought to be the uppermost of the Ceres coals, but the borings did not reach down to the Ceres Thick coal, which would have confirmed the suggestion. Three shafts were put down between North Callange and Kinninmonth in response to the borehole findings and at least one of these is known to have been working in 1853. Little detail of the workings at Kinninmonth are currently available, but there are early references by Dixon and Bell (1808) suggesting that some coals had been worked there by Andrew Watt around 1700, before being abandoned, and the shafts filled with wastes. These lands, formerly owned by the historian Lindsay of Pitscottie, were by this time owned by Sir Thomas Hope of Craighall.

One boring, near Coaltoun of Callange, found that the upper of the two coals worked by the Callange Coal Company lay three metres below the ground surface and the lower one was 68m beneath it. A 0.70m thick limestone lay between the two coals, at a depth of 46m. It is most likely that these two coals were the Ceres Black Coal below which was the Ballfield coal. This was the borehole which subsequently flooded the mine in 1877.

Landale (1837) made no more than passing reference to the fact that, between the Coaltown of Callange and Burnsquare (Nether Baldinnie), there was much evidence of former coal workings, long since abandoned by the time of his writing. His map of the coal seams is suitably ornamented with dotted lines to indicate their possible, but not proven continuations in that area. Today there are no exposures of the rocks to give more or less confidence in his predictions.

THE EASTERN COALFIELDS

A series of coalfields and limestone workings, situated on what are now just beyond the outskirts of St Andrews, were worked through much of the eighteenth century and, like those of Callange, well into the nineteenth century. The operations consisted of a collection of neighbouring but small and largely independent enterprises. In the north, the coalfields included workings at Lumbo, Mount Melville, Craigton, Claremont and Denork and in the south it stretches west from Denhead, through Winthank and Cassindonald, to Wilkieston. (Fig.8) The clusters of small coalfields lay between substantial fault lines. The northwest to southeast trending Radernie Fault marks the southwestern margin of these coalfields, beyond which are former workings at Northbank and Greigston; two closely spaced, almost east-west trending fractures, the Maiden Rock and Claremont Faults and their associated minor fractures form the northern limit. Within these boundaries are several lesser faults which not only cut through the coal-bearing succession, but also break across several of the intrusive dolerite sills. These faults, which have displaced the coal seams, effectively subdivide the eastern coalfield area into the smaller units. Thin igneous intrusions also line the fracture planes of some of the faults. As at Callange, several small volcanic necks are present, breaking through the sedimentary successions, including the coals. The fields in each of the fault-bounded units will be considered in turn.

In addition to the substantial faulting and intrusion the coals and limestones have been tilted northwestwards in the south. However, in the Denork-Claremont block, where the coals were worked into the late 1880s, the succession has been tilted eastwards. Near Denhead the succession has been folded into a tight symmetrical syncline with its axis in a north to south direction. Two small synclines with their axes trending northeast to southwest are present in the Kinness Burn at Lumbo Bridge and in its tributary, the Cairnsmill Burn at Cairnsmill.

The base of the Lower Limestone Formation coal-bearing succession in these coalfields is defined by the 3.5m thick St Monance Brecciated Limestone, which was formerly worked at Winthank, Cassindonald, Wilkieston, Denhead, Craigton Common and Lumbo. In addition to thin limestones and associated coals, the famous Blackband Ironstones were also worked from this south-eastern area. The ironstones, which were valuable iron ores, extended from Lumbo in the east through Denhead and Winthank to Cassindonald in the southwest, but rapidly thinned out westwards. They provided valuable industrial employment for a small work force between 1847 and 1866.

The ironstones and coals are interbedded at several localities, and extensive exploration for the ironstones served also to reveal the presence of viable coals. An account of the ironstones will follow consideration of the coals and coalfields. Along the eastern outcrop of this group of coalfields the limestones and coals are those of the Lower Limestone Formation, as also seen in the Radernie and Largoward coalfields to the south and south west. The Drumcarro Coalfield, within the same fault-bounded block as the Cassindonald succession, contains two groups of slightly younger coals, equated with the Ceres coals, in a sequence which terminates against the major fault defining the southeastern margin of Ladeddie Hill.

Winthank – Cassindonald

In 1885 Landale provided a summary of a series of reports which he had produced between the years of 1847 and 1866 on the coals and ironstones of the south-eastern coalfields. Each of the rock units identified in Table 4 was considered individually.

Target rocks	Thickness (m)	Other rocks	Thickness (m)	Total depth (m)
Little Splint	0.61			0.61
		Various strata	27.30	27.91
		Pelt, good roof	0.91	28.82
Largoward Parrot	1.0			29.82
Largoward Splint	0.61			30.43
		Various strata	20.12	50.55
Largoward Black	0.66			51.21
		Various strata	27.5	78.71
Mid-Kinniny Lst	1.50			80.21
		Shale	5.49	85.70
Coarse Parrot or Rum	0.38			86.08
		Shale	0.25	86.33
Charlestown Main Limestone	0.61			86.94
		Shale	0.43	87.37
Coal, poor, soft	0.51			87.88
		Fireclay, soft	2.54	90.42
Parrot Coal	0.15			90.57
Rums Coal	0.30			90.87
Blackband Ironstone	0.53			91.40
		Coaly Blaes	0.05	91.45
Ironstone Splint Coal	0.66			92.11
		Various strata	5.49	97.60
Low Little Coal	0.46			98.06
		Various strata	18.3	116.36
St.Monance Brecciated Lst	3.66			120.02

Table 4. The lower part of the Lower Limestone Formation rock succession in a pit shaft at Denhead village (based on Landale, 1847)

The uppermost coal seam in the areas of Winthank and Denhead is believed to be the equivalent of the Largoward Parrot and Largoward Splint coals which were separated by a very thin layer of shale. Elsewhere they have been referred to equally under either title, but in this work the combined coal will be referred to as the Largoward Parrot Coal. Both were thought of as excellent quality coals, breaking cleanly, easy to work and were well liked by the colliers. There was a good roof of pelt (bituminous shale) to the combined seam, which made the workings safe. Both coals were largely worked out before the Parrot Coals became prime targets following the development of town gas supplies, notably for St Andrews. We do know that the Parrot burned noisily, as is typical of such coals, and left a little clean white ash, known locally as 'ghaist' on residual surfaces.

The Largoward Black Coal is variously quoted as being up to 1.1metres in thickness. Its upper part was a good quality splint coal and the lower part a softer cherry or rough coal. In places it was expensive to work because it suffered from the presence of a poor roof to the seam, but in the Denhead area it was often found to have a fine strong roof.

Beneath the Mid-Kinniny Limestone lay a Coarse Parrot Coal which, although of marginally adequate quality, was too thin to be worked on its own. Likewise, below the Charlestown Main Limestone was a second, slightly thicker, soft coal which was worked locally for lime burning.

Above the Blackband Ironstone lay a Parrot Coal and a Rums Coal, both of which were worked for lime burning before the value of the ironstone was recognised. Indeed when the coals were being worked the pieces of ironstone were discarded as waste, and these underground heaps of rubbish, referred to as 'biggins', were later reworked when the focus of interest changed.

The Ironstone Coal, lying immediately below the Blackband Ironstone, was a relatively good coal, long worked for lime burning. It yielded mainly small pieces of material but relatively few great coals. A rather dirty coal, it also produced a white 'ghaist' on burning. It was too thin to work on its own, but was exploited when taken with the overlying ironstones. However the roof to these workings was very poor, especially where the rums near the top were thin. The exploitation of what was an unpredictable coal and the associated ironstones required that the spatial separation between the extraction shafts needed to be small.

The Low Little Coal, was a coarse, splint coal, which was mainly worked for lime burning and sometimes as an engine coal for nearby operations. It was at the minimum thickness limit for working (0.45m) and was taken only where drained (to 35m) by the Gowkston Day Level as its price at market did not justify the cost of engine-supported pumping. The 2.4 km long Gowkston Day Level had been brought into the area from the Denbrae area at no little expense during the eighteenth century. The Low Little Coal extends east to Feddinch but, although several attempts were made to exploit it, all proved unsuccessful. Worked by Sime at Cassindonald in 1870, it was later unsuccessfully prospected by several people, including Pryde who also had mining interest at this time in the New Gilston area.

Landale concluded that there was no known coal at Winthank that was of value for household purposes, or which would be able to compete in the market at St Andrews or elsewhere with the now available rail-borne coals. He noted that Messrs Merry and

Cunningham had undertaken a programme of borehole exploration in the Winthank area, but found no workable coals.

The coals towards the centre of the column in Table 4 were worked at Winthank and Denhead for a long period, as was the Little Coal, below them. Both the Rums and Splint were used for lime burning, principally with the thick St Monance Brecciated Limestone, which was worked nearby.

Lumbo and Mount Melville

The Lumbo-Mount Melville area lay just north of the limit of the pioneering Landale (1837) coalfield map, and as he was in close contact with the industry, it is assumed that no systematic active working was under way here at that time. However, in the first local map produced by the Geological Survey of Scotland in 1855, one coal seam was recognised at Lumbo Bridge and another was shown as crossing the upper part of the reservoir at Cairns Mill. The uppermost of three limestones below Cairns Mill was referred to as the Five Foot Limestone, which is commonly seen as being the equivalent of the Mid-Kinniny Limestone. It was worked for some years in the late eighteenth and early nineteenth centuries in quarries and, to a limited extent, it was also removed from below ground. Several outcrops of a parrot coal were shown as being present above the ironstones. The parrot coal was worked in at least two pits southwest of Lumbo. Both the ironstones and parrot coal have been folded into a syncline and a minor anticline, extending from Lumbo through Mount Melville. Discontinuous dolerite sills outcrop at many localities in this area and have been quarried for building materials. Geikie (1902) drew attention to an ingaunee which penetrated below one dolerite sill in search of coal and limestone, but stressed that no economic working had been carried on in that area for many years.

During searches for coal and ironstone deposits, at least eleven boreholes were reported to have been put down in the Lumbo, Feddinch and Mount Melville area. Most found 'troubled' conditions suggesting the presence of faults, but several did prove the presence of the ironstones, with their associated thin coals, usually of dubious quality, at depth. The locations of several boreholes from the 1850s are known along the crest of the small Lumbo anticline. One which reached down to 97m indicated the presence of the thin ironstone, but found no workable coal. A second borehole, 80m deep encountered a parrot coal 0.84m thick at 37m. About 800m to the southwest a 27.4m deep borehole of the Geological Survey at the former Craigtoun Hospital found that below the base of the dolerite sill no less than six coal seams up to 0.5m in thickness, are present, although all were marginally unworkable, In the 60m deep Craigtoun Park No 1 borehole, which crossed a fault at shallow depth, there were four coals thicker than 0.6m at levels down to 51m. Forsyth and Chisholm (1977) believed these to be younger than the coals in the Hospital borehole. The uppermost, 2.8m thick, coal was tentatively equated with the Ceres Thick coal. The three seams below the fault were believed to be the equivalents of layers within the Four Foot and Five Foot Coals of Ceres. In a second borehole in Craigtoun Park two coals 0.84m and 1.02m thick, believed to be the lower layer of the Five Foot Coal and the Ceres Thick coal respectively, were located above the dolerite sill. However, none of these coals has been proved at the surface, and although there remain signs of some historic surface workings for the coals no detail is known of their exploitation.

In 1855 Landale reported that a deep pit put down on the Feddinch grounds had also drained a shallower pit near Lumbo. In both mines the rocks were broken along many small faults. Patches of high quality ironstone increased to thicknesses of 0.25-0.40m towards the Feddinch steading, but vanished to the west, where the often steeply inclined rocks were very 'troubled'. Two years later, a cross-cut mine from Feddinch linked with the Lumbo workings where fifteen men worked in the thin, rather poor quality Little Coal beneath the ironstone.

This coal was used entirely to fuel the engine driving the pumps at Feddinch. It was only by working the coal and the ironstone from the same location that the enterprise was economically viable. Unfortunately the pit shaft was positioned on a fault which carried much water into the workings, dangerously weakening a fireclay layer. In a further working by the road east of the Lumbo steading, six men are known to have worked in 0.53m thick troubled ironstones which dipped at one in three. One year later, in 1858, Landale noted that as a result of the great depression in the Iron Trade and the cost of buying limestone, the Lochgelly Iron Co. Ltd. had given their year's notice to quit both Lumbo and Feddinch, but he urged that the pits should be left open and walled round in case others might return to the workings at a later date.

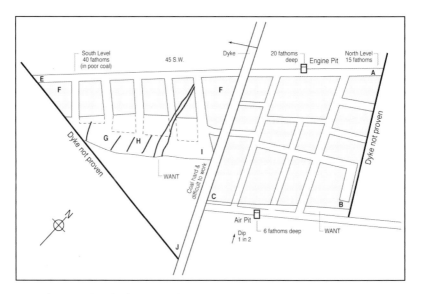

Fig. 13. Sketch of coal workings at Mount Melville, (after Landale 1866)

As at Lumbo, the structural disposition of the beds was somewhat confused near Mount Melville. Generally, where seen, the layers of rock including the coal seams were inclined at low angles, but in no consistent direction. The very disturbed nature of the visible rocks led Landale (1866) to believe that at least one major fault crossed the area near Mount Melville house, and lesser faults with 5.5m to 8m displacements were marked on the early survey maps. The tenants of the coal lease, Miller and Nelson sank a 36m deep pit to a 1.2m thick Parrot Coal. The heavily watered and steeply southward-dipping (one in two) seam was composed of two 0.3m thick layers of rough common coal above and below a similar thickness of good gas coal. Unusually for this area the seam also incorporated a 0.3m thick layer of oil shale.

In the absence of a plan of the workings, Landale (1866) provided a sketch of the layout (Fig 13). He showed the main 36m deep level aligned NE-SW encountering a WNW-ESE trending fault (AB) some 27m NE of the pit shaft. Despite exploration, no coal had been found beyond the fault. About 14m SW of the shaft, the level encountered a thick dolerite dyke (CD) intruded along a fault with a downthrow of at least 1.5m to the southwest. Following the same line (DE) the level was cut for 73m along more coal until it met a further fault (EJ), this time trending E-W, beyond which attempts were then being made to locate a continuation of the coal.

The quality of the coal in the panel ABCD was good, although the seam ended in an unexplained want a little short of the 13m deep Air Pit (K) along the line BC. In the second panel DEJ the coals were of lesser quality, often troubled and foul, exceptions being in pillars at F and E. Ongoing longwall workings at G,H, and I were also in poor coals which were harder towards the central dyke. A second want was recorded trending N-S between I and H, broadening southwards. Only the small triangle (IJG) of working area remained for extraction at that time.

Claremont-Denork

About 250m to the north of the road between St Andrews and Claremont the eastward flowing Claremont Burn occupies the floor of a deep narrow gully. Within the wooded land, immediately beside the St Andrews road is an opening from which waters flow freely to join the burn. Contrary to its appearance the point of issue is not a spring, but the lower end of the 2.4km long Gowkston Day Level, an important drainage structure built in the early eighteenth century and refurbished and extended on several occasions over the next hundred and fifty years.. Unlike the Callange day level, the lower section of which was culverted and buried some time after its excavation, the lower reaches of the Gowkston day level remain open well into the uphill slope of the land. The Day Level drains much of the western part of the lands of Craigton Common, in which there were small coal and limestone workings belonging to James Nairn of Claremont. It also drained the Claremont and Denork coalfields northeast of Drumcarrow Craig, and part of the Denhead-Winthank coal and ironstone workings, to the southeast.

According to an eye-sketch provided in 1822 by James McLaren (Fig.7), the Gowkston Day Level followed the line of the excavated ravine east of Elderburn Farm (sometimes referred to as Wester Denhead), continuing across the line of the track between Elderbank and Denhead before deflecting to the southwest and passing almost directly beneath the road junction at Denhead Farm. McLaren indicated the locations of a series of ventilation pits to the day level. South of pit No. 5 the day level encountered the combined Largoward Parrot and Splint coal and diverted in its path to follow it southwestwards to beneath the cross-roads, where at that time it terminated against a large east-west trending fault. Later it was carried still farther southwards. The 5m diameter Pit shaft No. 8 remains identifiable today between the road and the house of the Drumcarrow Livery Company.

By 1839, Landale supplemented McLaren's report, providing detail of the coal seams to the south of a dolerite dyke intruded along a large east-west trending fault which crosses the Strathkinness to Colinsburgh road a short distance north of the sharp double bend (Fig.8). Here the four coals recognised as dipping east-southeastwards were considered by Gemmel (1900) to be the same coals as identified below the Largoward Black Coal in the Winthank-Cassindonald area.

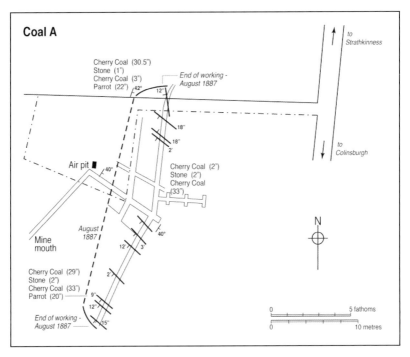

Fig 14a. Sketch of coal workings in Coal A , the Scrumpie
Coal at Denork, (after Landale 1889)

However, a substantial fault is present terminating the Denhead syncline at its northern end and also the four Claremont coals in their southern extremity. The lower three of these coals which pass beneath the Gowkston Day Level to the north of the fault may be unrelated to the succession of rocks in the Denhead syncline. It is suggested here that, in the absence of the prominent limestones, the four Claremont coals are the equivalents of the Lower part of the Ceres coal succession, albeit here dipping below the Craigton Common and Mount Melville areas. Colliers who were last in the pits in 1797 indicated to McLaren (1822) that the northernmost shaft (Pit No.1) led down through sandstones before encountering the wastes from a 1.5m thick coal at 36m.

The gas rich coal wastes, believed to have been from a Parrot coal were full of bad air and had been worked out at that site at a much earlier date. The 44m deep Pit No. 1 was on the Day Level, at the boundary between the lands of Claremont and those of Craigton Common. North of the fault line this uppermost coal, identified by Landale as A was the low quality 'Scrumpie' Coal seam. Landale believed that this was one of the seams that MacRitchie, an early tacksman, had worked.

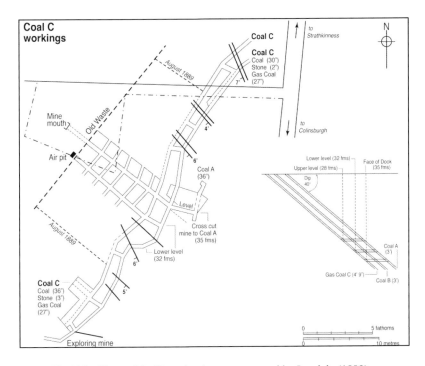

Fig.14 b. Plans of the Denork mines as surveyed by Landale (1889),
showing the principal working roads in Coal C. The inserted
cross section indicates the eastward dipping seams
and the relative positions of the workings

A second seam B, which outcrops a short distance to the west, was the 1.2m thick Cave Coal. This much higher quality cherry and splint coal with a yellow sandstone roof dips at a gradient of one in two eastwards. It was successfully worked by entering from the side of the ravine and creating a level to the north of Pit No. 1, continuing the level southwards to a little west of West Denhead and working to the rise. The third seam, C, outcrops at the double bend on the road to Strathkinness. Although it lacks a formal name locally, this extensively worked seam was generally referred to as 'the gas coal.' It was initially exploited from the low lands in 'Durham's Park' at Claremont where it, too, had a yellow sandstone roof. The fourth seam D, was recorded as some 2.1m thick locally. There is little more known of it beyond the fact that it was worked and that, in the 1850s, fragments of parrot coal were said to have been found along its supposed surface outcrop.

In the north, the three coal seams B, C and D were all worked, but only as shallow mines, penetrating no deeper than an early day level from the low lands of Claremont, nearly 22m above the level of the Gowkston Day Level. In 1839, there was a proposal to open up the lower levels beneath the Claremont lands by creating a cross-cutting stone mine from Pit No. 1.

At that time it was known that the Gowkston Day Level was in a poor state of repair and could be cleared only at some expense, as the workings progressed. The early workings of this phase of activity were funded by selling coals recovered from the biggins, residual infilling wastes, from the much earlier mining. Although the bulk of the coalfield to the north had been exhausted by the 1850s, Landale considered that there was more coal to be exploited from the lands of Denork, to the south, using the levels derived from such a stone mine. However, he suggested limiting the tenants to working east of a line from Denork Farm Steading to Andrew Guillon's tomb (location not currently known, perhaps a collapsed shaft) at least until all the coals had been removed down to the position of the Gowkston level. Whether this extension was undertaken is not known. After 1883, when further exploratory boreholes were put down west of the Strathkinness-Colinsburgh road, the lease was taken up by Hurl and Jack, who created drift mines through the old surface wastes west of the road and cleaned out the Gowkston Day Level between Pits Nos. 1 and 2. However, they gave up the lease early, concluding that the coals in the remaining seams were unfit for sale. The proprietor, Mr. Ireland, reworked some of the wastes of both seams B and D and cleaned out some of the earlier pits, but he died soon thereafter. The only known lessee thereafter was a Mr. Neilson from Glasgow, but he soon abandoned the workings.

Of two plans of the Denork mines collected by Landale, both dated 1889, (Figs 14a and b) the first shows the worked area of Coal A dipping south-eastwards at 40°. The second plan, refers to the worked area of Coal C and indicates the routes of cross-cut mines to coals B and A, 8m and 21m respectively above coal C. Neither plan shows a coal as thick as the sometimes claimed 2.1m thickness for Coal D. Once the workings extended to the lands of Denork, south of Claremont, drift mines were developed to the northwest of Wester Denhead. Along the outcrop substantial old mine wastes were present as the original workings at Denork had been from the surface. However, beyond a depth of 15m the working of coal C was from six northeast to southwest trending levels, the lowest of which reached 70m below the surface. The individual panels were removed by longwall techniques. Plans prepared in 1887 showed that the total workings from the drift mines west of the Strathkinness to Colinsburgh Road had extracted panels of coal A from approximately 100m by 25m, and coal C from panels totalling approximately 150m by 60m, beneath an area of approximately 0.9 hectares in the Denork grounds. In 1880 Landale calculated that the extraction of the Cave Coal (coal B) and five feet of the Cherry Coal (coal D) over an area of 12 hectares would yield some 180,000 tons of saleable coals, yielding a sum of £4500 to the estate lordship (one ninth of the sales value). At this time he estimated that the accessible reserves would last for a further twenty years unless a projected railway route nearby, with inevitable increase in demand for production that that would stimulate, was to be built. However, there is no evidence that extraction was attempted over such a period, and there may still be reserves at depth in these grounds.

The coals continued southwards from Claremont until cut off along the east to west trending fault EF south of Wester Denhead, within the lands of Denork. In the north the coals were cut off along a second substantial east-west fault dubbed GH.

Denhead – Gowkston

To the east of Elderbank, and north and west of the Winthank area, lies a succession of coals and limestones which stretch to stratigraphic levels above those given in Table 4. From the eastern outcrop near Winthank Overtown the rocks slope northwestwards at dips of one in five, but the angle steepens to one in two before reaching the Strathkinness-Colinsburgh road. A short way east of the Denhead Farm road junction, the beds flatten and rapidly reverse their dips as they assume equally steep inclinations towards the southeast. Lines of irregular surface features are still visible leading northeast along the worked outcrops of two coal seams, the Largoward Black Coal and, 16.5m above it, the combined Largoward Splint and Parrot coals. The two coals were both worked along the outcrops of this sharply defined and relatively narrow Denhead syncline. McLaren (1822) indicated the locations of a series of ventilation pits thrown up from the Gowkston Day Level (Fig.7). Between pits Nos. 5 and 6, as indicated above, the day level encountered the Largoward Parrot coal and diverted southwestwards, following the coal to beneath the cross-roads, where it terminated against a large east-west trending fault. A cross-cut stone mine from the day level in the Largoward Parrot coal followed a northwest-southeast direction intersecting both the Black and Parrot coals on both limbs of the syncline. Later two lines of pit shafts, constructed by Taylor, led down to the 44m level worked on both limbs of the fold, from which the coals were taken to the rise.

The western limb of the syncline emerged into the area between Drumcarrow Craig and the Strathkinness to Colinsburgh road, in fields which currently show a heavily disrupted surface, with, amongst other features, raised ridges around the tops of former access shafts. Some of the tops, which are circular and rarely more than three metres across, are marked on the Ordnance Survey maps. There are at least two sets of shafts aligned approximately northeast to southwest, along the direction of strike of the western limb of the syncline. One of the best preserved shaft tops, in the grounds of the Drumcarrow Livery stables and adjacent to the cross-road, is 4-5m across and surrounded by a raised rim more than a meter in height. This particular shaft is on the line of the Gowkston day level and may be an enlargement of Air Pit No. 8 on McLaren's map of 1822. The tops nearest the road were used for access to the Largoward Parrot Coal and those further west and beyond the field boundary were on the Largoward Black Coal.

In the early 1840s, there were proposals to deepen the mine and construct a cross-cut mine to the level of the base of the trough to enable the all of the coals to be worked to the rise on each limb of the fold, but these suggestions were rejected on the grounds of economy, as relatively little additional coal from the base of the syncline would have been accessed. As the drainage waters would have needed to be pumped into the Gowkston Day Level by a steam engine, the cost was deemed too great for the potential return and the proposal was abandoned. In a report dated 25th January1847, Landale indicated that the Largoward Parrot and the Largoward Black coals had by then all been worked at Denhead to a depth of 46m, and confirmed that that left only relatively small quantities of coal in the ground at the base of the syncline.

In a manuscript report by Dott (1941) reference is made to the belief of Gemmell (1900) that the Gowkston Coals are about 61m below the Drumcarro Coals at Denhead and 91m above the Winthank Coals. The grounds for this assertion are not clear.

McLaren records that it was not until Pit No. 5 was put down (Fig.7) that the Largoward Parrot coal was entered, and Landale (1839) suggested that the presence of an east to west trending fault near the line of the Denhead to Elderbank Smithy road would account for the apparent absence of the seams further north. However, both may be present in discontinuous outcrops in the Mount Melville-Lumbo area.

Drumcarro

The Drumcarro coalfield area extended from the upper reaches of the Kinninmonth Burn immediately north of Cassindonald and as far north as the southern slopes of Drumcarrow Craig and Ladeddie Hill. (Fig.8) Its coals are of the Limestone Coal Formation and the upper part of the Lower Limestone Formation. The position of the boundary marker between the two stratigraphic divisions, namely the Upper Kinniny Limestone and its associated Marl Coal (the Ballfield Coal of Ceres) is conjectural, neither being known at outcrop or in boreholes in this area. The Drumcarro coals will be considered separately from the coals, limestones and ironstones of the Cassindonald-Winthank area, which are of the lower part of the Lower Limestone Formation of sediments. The southwestern limit of the coalfield is formed by the northwest-southeast trending Ladeddie Fault, which crosses the line of the road mid-way between Drumcarro Farm and Ladeddie Steading. In practice there were actually two sets of workings in the Drumcarro coalfield, one in the west towards the boundary of the grounds with those of Ladeddie and the other north of Drumcarro Farm.A cross-section of the western workings at Drumcarro (Fig 14) is based on a plan by Landale in 1841, which indicates the layers dipping towards the northwest, more steeply near the surface than at depth. As with the early exploitation of most of the local areas the coal outcrops were worked long before plans of the sites were produced. With the sun at a suitably low angle, discontinuous lines of hollows marking the outcrops or shallow collapse structures along the lines of the principal worked coal outcrops may sometimes be detected on the surface today between Drumcarro Farm Steading and Drumcarrow Craig, north of the present road. The earliest records show that in the early eighteenth century Calderwood Durham of Largo identified the outcrops of several of the seams at Drumcarro and extended the former coal workings at and downwards from the surface. He opened up a series of drift mines to follow the coals, which were generally inclined northwestward at dip angles of around 25 degrees.

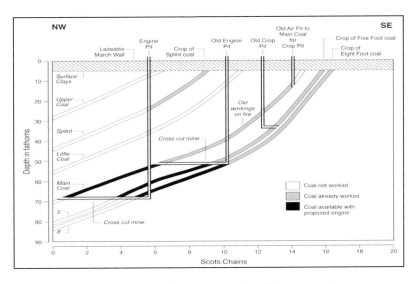

Fig.15. A northwest to southeast cross-section of the western Drumcarro
Workings indicating levels to which the coals had been worked from the
surface, the Crop Pit, the Old Engine Pit and the Engine Pit. Note the
decreasing dip of the coal seams with depth (after Landale, 1841).
The thicknesses of the seams are not shown to scale

By the time that Melville and Archibald visited the area in 1753, they were aware of
the existence of six seams in the Drumcarro grounds, the thickest and youngest being
towards the west. They recommended that a series of shafts or boreholes be put down well
to the east of the Drumcarro-Ladeddie March wall which separated the two properties,
indicating that the shafts should reach at least a depth of 14-16.5m. From knowledge of
the depths to a particular seam at several places the direction of strike (the horizontal line
within the coal) could be determined. This would provide a guide to the direction along
which the levels would need to be constructed below ground for draining and working the
coals.

The earliest recorded pit put down on the main western Drumcarro coal workings was
the 60m deep Crop Pit 200m south of the eastern end of Smithy Row Cottages, from where
at least the Five Foot coal was taken to the rise, and may have linked with the drift mine
wastes from above. The Five Foot coal was also worked from a second early shaft, the
Dean Pit, situated about 100m north of the eastern end of Smithy Row Cottages. The
remains of these cottages currently occupy the stretch of woodland east of Drumcarro
Westfield House. The dates of operating of neither of these pits are known, but
presumably both substantially predated the report by Melville and Archibald in 1753 as
they were no longer in use at that time.

In 1801, Robert Punshon reported to Captain Rigg, owner of the Drumcarro lands, that

Durham was at that time working the 1.2m thick Splint Coal at Drumcarro in an area near the march dyke (wall) with Ladeddie. He had previously used a steam engine at a depth of 91 m to service the Main Coal, and access both the Five Foot and Eight Foot seams by cross-cutting eastwards from this level to below the Smithy Row Cottages. This was the Old Engine Pit, located 25m south of the road and 175m south southwest of the western end of the Smithy Row Cottages. At a depth of 91m, it entered the Eight Foot Coal, having already penetrated the Little Coal, the Main Coal and the Five Foot Coal. All three of these lower coals were worked to the rise, from levels constructed from the base of the Old Engine Pit. In working the Five Foot and Eight Foot Coals however, the colliers met with old wastes much sooner than had been anticipated (there being no plan of the abandoned old workings available), and the average breadth of the coals gained was only about 22m. The limited additional ground which was available for working led to the tenants breaking the terms of their agreement and halving the required 12m of protective barrier between the new and the old workings. In order to protect their own workings the manager had the colliers build stoppings with stones and clay to keep out drainage waters. They entered the lower sections of the old workings of both the Five Foot and Eight Foot seams and removed a substantial volume of material from both. Access to the Five Foot seam from shallower workings extending downwards from the surface had previously been given up due to a fire becoming established in the seam. The Five Foot Coal in the older workings was sufficiently gassy to permit combustion to continue, and an extension to the slow burning fire from this seam became established in the new workings when the colliers opened a connection between the new and old sections of the mine. Over a period of several years of this new phase of extraction the fire's slow advance was carefully monitored as the previously untouched coals continued to be worked. Fresh stoppings were emplaced and water pumped into the burning side to impede and slow the forward advance of the fire.

The fire advanced at a sufficiently slow rate to permit continued extraction of the coal in advance of the burning, which impacted the roof, pavement and support pillars. Despite setting up stoppings to separate the working areas from the fire, the smoke and lack of good air led to many problems for the work force. In the Report of the Government Commission on the Employment of Young People in Mines (1842) verbatim comments from several of the Drumcarro workers were provided, Alexander Smith, a hewer, aged 14, stated that the so-called 'stifle' could cause the hewers or their supporters to fall unconscious at their places of work. Their colleagues would then "take them up into the fresh air, which brings them back to their senses."

In calm warm summer weather conditions when there was little motion of the air above the workings the mines were not uncommonly kept closed on account of the build-up of the stifle conditions. Ventilation induced by the heat from the engine boilers at the foot of the main shaft drawing in fresh air from ventilation shafts elsewhere in the workings was insufficient to reach the more remote parts of the workings, and a plan dated 1836 shows the presence of only two air pits on the Drumcarro grounds, one 350m from the northernmost part, and the other in the extreme south of the property. As the workings were extended northwards a series of faults were encountered, each throwing the coals up by a few metres on their northern side, with the faults becoming more closely spaced towards the terminal fault, beside the face of Drumcarrow Craig. Recognising that the operations on the seams were coming to an end it was decided to remove part of the supporting coal pillars as activity was withdrawn towards the shaft. Some of the more important pillars were preserved, and even given protection against the progressive fire. This led to disputes with some of the colliers, who saw the leaving of pillars as wasting the potentially easily extracted material which would require little working for their production. In a visit late in 1841 Landale was asked to meet with one hewer who had become greatly agitated at the thought of abandoning such material. The discussions must have become heated as they ended with Landale making a firm recommendation that the hewer be discharged.

[It is interesting to note that the hewer concerned was a Mr Carlow. Whether he was related to Charles Carlow, a mining engineer who became Principal Manager of the Fife Coal Company in 1877, and later its very successful Chairman, is not known. At a later date, in 1896, Charles Carlow's nephew, Mr. C. Augustus Carlow, also became a valued Director of the Company. (Muir, 1958)]

The Five Foot Coal was worked directly from the level of the base of the Old Engine Pit. It was linked eastwards to the Eight Foot Coal by a cross-cut mine and also similarly linked westwards to the Main Coal seam. Access and drainage levels in each seam extended as far north as the bounding faults along the foot of Drumcarrow Craigs. The waters from above the level of the Old Engine Pit were discharged into a ditch which led southwards into the Kinninmonth Burn.

Two pits about 49m deep are known to have been taken down separately to the Splint Coal. These gave access to a limited volume of recoverable coal as they were worked to the rise and at best would have encountered the base of the surficial glacial tills at depths of no less than 4.5m, assuming that no earlier outcrop workings were present.

In a report, dated 25th April 1801, Robert Punshon of the Wemyss Company advised Mr. Thomson of Charleton, the then owner, that virtually all of the accessible coals above the position of the Old Engine Pit levels had already been removed by that date. However, Mr Durham was at that time working a one metre thick coal (probably the Splint Coal) in the lands of Drumcarro in an area adjacent to the march dyke with Ladeddie. He was proposing to extend the mines westward by driving a linkage beneath the lands of Ladeddie to reach an area of two acres (0.8ha) of this same coal, and drain it using the pumping capacity of the existing engine in the Old Engine Pit. Punshon believed that this should be agreed to, and, estimated that, at seven shillings a ton selling price, this would bring in some £1250 per acre to the seller. He suggested that Mr. Thomson should ask for a royalty of one twelfth of this sum, bearing in mind the costs that Durham would incur in needing to drive the 146m stone mine in strong rocks. It was also pointed out that by the date of the report all of the other accessible coals above the position of the Drumcarro level had already been removed, so this would be the last phase of working from the main Drumcarro colliery.

There is no indication of when this development took place. However, soon after 1800, a second Engine Pit was created 30m south of the Drumcarro-Denhead roadway 320m northwest of the Old Engine Pit and this provided a second level for working the Splint

Coal at 42m and also gave direct access to the Main Coal at 97m. The early workings of the Main Coal northward from the base of this Engine Pit revealed a series of at least five small, but continuous northwest to southeast trending faults which showed consistent upward movement on their northern side. All three coals were worked in 15-22m long panels by means of relatively narrow rooms 4.5m wide, with substantial pillars up to 9m broad separating them. This second Engine Pit enabled the mining to continue for more than thirty productive years before more substantial development was needed.

In 1838, Durham proposed to deepen the second Engine Pit by another 27m until it reached beyond the Five Foot Coal at 111m and into the Eight Foot Coal at 119m and so release direct access to a further extractable breadth of 70-90m of both of the lower coals. Importantly, in addition he also sought to drive a stone mine westwards to create a further linkage to the Main Coal beneath the landage of Ladeddie, to enable more of this coal to be extracted. Some form of agreement was reached between the two estates before such an enterprise could go ahead. It is interesting to note that this was not the first proposal to extract Ladeddie coals from the Drumcarro side of the March wall.

In December 1841, Landale wrote that the Drumcarro Coal Company wished to close down its workings in the following year. At that time a few colliers were removing much of the support pillars and building fire stoppings behind them in each seam as they retreated. All of the solid coals were to be removed within a year, including some at the base of the Engine Pit, which would need to remain open until all of the coals extending beneath the grounds of Ladeddie had been removed, once agreement with Captain Thomson had been reached. It appears that the agreement was concluded successfully because, in 1850, Landale observed that the west workings at Drumcarro were then coming to an end and that the day level barriers and crop pillars had been let to John Latto and Company, a group of the colliers, for their removal. The top of the 122m deep main shaft to the Drumcarro pit was capped by a masonry structure seen today in the garden to the west of Drumcarro Westfield House.

This group of workers put down a pit to the east of the Smithy Row houses, the remains of which, as noted previously, are today seen in the wooded area to the east of Drumcarro Westfield House. They reached the wastes of the Thick Main Coal but found them showing signs of being near the fire, so they closed up the level sides of the pit and cross-cut eastwards, reaching both the Five Foot and Eight Foot seams. In the latter they found large residual pillars and a lot of coarse coals which had been rejected by Durham and his earlier workers. They proceeded to sell this material and continued into the Five Foot coal, which turned out to be of better quality than expected. Four colliers worked north in this seam and then cut back into the Thick Main Coal of even better quality, but to the south the evidence of the fire was strong and after a fatality due to the bad air a new air pit was put down. The entire cost of this working was £200 and the income from the sales of the coals was recorded as £1003.

In accounts given to members of the Parliamentary Commission (1842) concerning children working in mines, Alexander Felfor, overseer of the Drumcarro mine indicated that of about fifty employees of the mine some fifteen were below the age of eighteen, with nine boys less than fourteen. He indicated that he considered very young people, below the age of twelve years, to be of little use in the mine as great care was needed on account of the fire hazard. As far as he knew at that time no females or very young children worked underground anywhere in the St. Andrews district. Up to that time, no serious accidents had taken place from the stifle. Many of the colliers had previously worked as agricultural labourers. Andrew Fernes, aged seventeen, had worked in the mines from the age of fourteen, having previously worked in the fields. In farm service he earned 4s1d per year plus bed and board, whereas in the mine he could earn 2/6 to 3/- per day. However he noted that the work was much harder and for consistently longer hours in the mines.

In 1853, Forrester opened up what was referred to as the Drumcarro colliery to the east of and uphill from the farm buildings. Unfortunately no detailed plans appear to exist of these workings, which exploited the same three seams as those worked to the west, viz. the Main, Five Foot, and Eight Foot Coals. A shaft descending to 38m a short way south of the road gave access to the Eight Foot Coal, which was reported as being 'a good coker.' A second shaft equally spaced to the north of the road was a 23m deep engine pit from which the Five Foot and Eight Foot Coals were worked, and to the north a 122m pit extended down to the Main Coal. Close to Drumcarrow Craig, the Eight Foot coal was noted as being steeply inclined, but had been worked for 14m down dip, using a small engine to evacuate the waters. In 1855, Landale commented that, although Forrester was seeking to employ more men at that time, there was little more room for expansion of the workings either to the north or to the south. Early maps suggest that the Main Coal outcrop may have passed towards Hillside House and those of the other two coals met the path between Hillside House and Brayside. The coal deposits terminate against the dolerite intrusion, with a strong contrast in land use being marked across the track which separates open cultivated fields on the coal-bearing rocks from the whin covered hillside on the intrusion. Towards the crest of the hill the track follows a small curve to the east, diverting round the position where the Collier's Hall stood during the exploitation of the mines. In the fields immediately below the former buildings the early maps suggest the presence of several old pits. These would have been upon the Three Foot Coal, which was at shallow depth in that area. With no plans to indicate any pattern of working here it is suggested that the six features marked were probably the tops of access-pits rather than bell-pits.

In a memorandum dated 23rd August 1900, Gemmel commented on the quality of the Largoward Black and Parrot coals noting that below the local day level these two coals remained untouched over a large area of the Drumcarro lands and suggested that, although at some depth, they could still have been worked profitably. However, there is no indication that this suggestion was ever followed up.

South of the dyke-lined east-west trending fault to the east of Drumcarrow Craig and the workings of Forrester, many old shafts of bell pits were noted as being present in 1822. They were said to have been remnants of workings on the Rum Coal and Little Coal, both of which had been recovered for lime burning. This is entirely possible on stratigraphic grounds. Neither coal was considered of great value, and McLaren recommended selling this part of the landage.

The only remaining coal bing of waste materials known to be present in this part of NE Fife is to the southeast of Drumcarro Farm steading, where the wastes of the Four Foot and Six Foot coals are thought to have been deposited, beside a small neck of volcanic rocks identified by the Geological Survey.

Backfield of Ladeddie

On the northwestern outcrop of the syncline, at Backfield of Ladeddie, the St Monance Brecciated Limestone was worked in open quarries and shallow mines. Above it, the flat lying equivalent of the Low Little Coal, known locally as the Two Foot Coal, was worked for lime burning. Three other seams, six, four and eleven feet thick respectively, situated among a series of faults, and dipping very steeply to the southeast were also worked for lime burning. The outcrop patterns of the stronger rocks and the intervening faults may be seen on the hillside to the east of the farm of Backfield of Ladeddie. However, the stratigraphic section, so clearly revealed on the southern limb of the strongly asymmetrical syncline, was heavily broken here, and large parts of the rock succession appear to be missing, at least partly due to the faulting.

In the 1753 report by William Melville and James Archibald, reference is made to the coal of this part of the Ladeddie estate, and there was a later report by Maclean, in 1818. A sketch map produced by James Ballingal in MacLean's report shows the path of a day level to the southeast of the main limestone quarry, indicating where the level discharged into an open drain leading towards Streamside of Blebo. The positions of four pits along the length of the stone mine in addition to several shaft tops and borehole sites from later explorations are shown on the modified map in Fig.16.

In 1855 Brown, from the Largoward Colliery, sought to exploit the three steeply dipping edge seams of coal and sank a shaft 44m deep to work them, proposing to use a separate day level, also to Streamside of Blebo for drainage of the Two Foot workings. The position of this drain has been added to the above map. However, the area of coals remaining beneath the set of earlier workings was small and the rocks were heavily faulted and intruded by dolerites. Once the residual coal pillars had been removed the workings were abandoned. It was estimated that Brown lost about £1000 on the enterprise.

Efforts to locate the presence of the Blackband Ironstones and exploitable deposits of coal in this area continued, and more exploratory boreholes were put down by several prospectors. In 1883 David Ireland, one of the last of these, drilled three boreholes in the westernmost field of the Denork lands, northwest of Ladeddie Hill. However, none of these encountered the ironstones, and only thin coals were found. On the north side of Ladeddie Hill, again thin coals were located. Although one potentially valuable deposit of parrot coal was identified, it had been substantially altered by the heat from the nearby intrusions and was deemed to be unworkable.

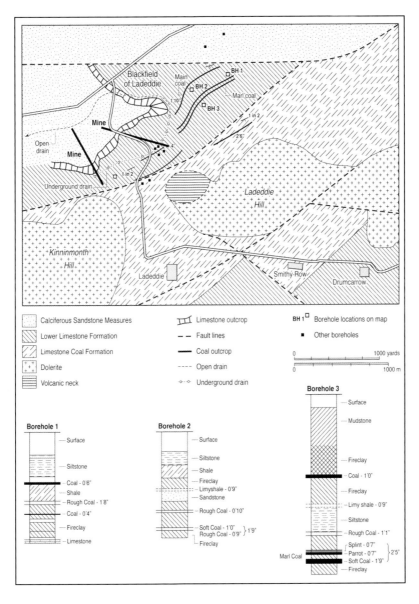

Fig.16. Geological map of the Backfield of Ladeddie coalfield,
after Ballingal (in MacLean 1818)

Ladeddie Colliery

The coals of the Ladeddie estate occur in two blocks of terrain straddling the northwest to southeast trending Ladeddie Fault which crosses the road mid-way between Drumcarro Farm and Ladeddie. To the north is a small area with the uppermost part of the succession already discussed in relation to developments of the Drumcarro coalfield, namely the Main Coal, and the overlying Splint Coal. Above these one foul coal and a parrot coal are known to be present, and on a plan of the Drumcarro workings dating from when the excavation of the Main Coal from the second level had progressed no more than 108m from the base of the pit (possibly about 1810?), two long-disused shaft tops are marked 70m and 120m north of the roadway and 60m west of the March dyke separating the two estates. A third shaft is also marked 70m north of the road and 130m from the March dyke. It is probable that the upper, unnamed parrot coal was taken from these pits and also the Splint coal, which would have been at a depth of no more than 55m in the shafts to the west of the march dyke.

To the south of the road, and on the southern side of the fault, the succession differs greatly, with two coals exploited. Although very restricted in lateral extent, these appear to be the equivalents of the coals worked in the east of the Drumcarro block by Forrester, namely the Largoward Parrot and either the Little Splint or the lower Four Foot Coal. The upper seam in the Ladeddie workings exceeds 1m in thickness only in the extreme north of the mine. If, indeed, these are the two coals seen to the northeast there has been a considerable reduction in the thickness of the intervening sedimentary rocks between the coals.

Although the principal seams worked towards the end of the life of the coalfield are those listed above, there is evidence from the outfalls of day levels and the tops of long-disused shafts that the area to the south-east had supported mining some time before the operations began in the Drumcarro and Ladeddie districts. The presence of a former shaft top and a suspected day level outfall to a burn suggest that extraction may have taken place from the Largoward Black Coal from the shaft, but there are neither records nor outcrops to permit confirmation of which seam, if any, was worked.

Once agreement had been reached that the Main Coal had been exhausted an effort was made to establish whether the Four Foot (1.22m) coal known to be present elsewhere above the Main Thick Coal might also be present on the margins of Ladeddie Hill. Trial pits did locate a 0.71m thick Parrot coal, but it was in a substantially altered state as a result of its proximity to the dolerite sill, to the extent that it was very difficult to ignite. No further workings were pursued to the north of the road. Records of the National Mining Museum show that in 1912 an exploratory drilling was put down to the south of the road, within the present grounds of Wester Drumcarro house, to the west of the now derelict Smithy Row Cottages. The findings of that exploration are not known.

Ladeddie Colliery (South)

The Ladeddie Colliery came into operation in 1858, after Brown had abandoned his workings at Backfield of Ladeddie. It was not the first colliery in these grounds, for on putting down boreholes and pits, it was found that there were substantial masses of coal wastes at several localities. Evidently former colliers had worked the coals from the surface before moving elsewhere. The new colliery, in the fields south-east of the Ladeddie steading (Fig.17), was operational between 1858 and 1863. Here the rocks lie to the south of the Ladeddie Fault and appear to be confined to the upper part of the Lower Limestone Formation succession, To the east exposures of what was termed a Parrot Coal dipping northwest at fourteen degrees showed a succession with 0.3m of rough coals beneath 0.1m of black fireclay leading to 0,13m of a gas coal and a further 0.13m of splint coals below a yellow sandstone roof. (Fig. 17)

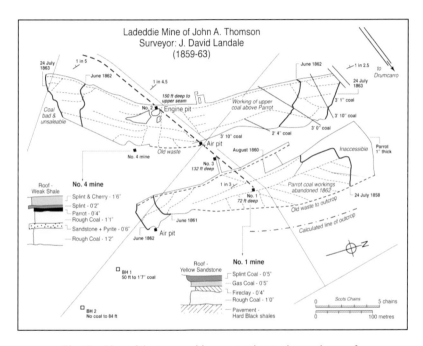

Fig.17. Plan of the two workings operating to the southeast of
Ladeddie steading in the period 1858-1863

81

The gas coal was of top quality and sold at the very good price of 19/- per ton on the hill. Unfortunately this part of the seam thinned both to north and south and also down dip. The seam was opened up by a shaft 40m deep. In 1859, Landale reported that the workings to the north of the shaft were providing six longwall sections, but only one to the south. By 1862 maps of the workings show that for various reasons the northern section of the coals had become inaccessible, mainly through thinning, and in the south two longwall operations had become very restricted as the coals also thinned in that direction. The workings were described as level free, i.e. they drained naturally down the dip direction, and no pumping was needed. This colliery, thought to have been on the combined Largoward Splint and Parrot Coal, ceased working in 1863.

A second seam of parrot coal, 1.5m thick, with gas coals at the top outcropped to the west. A new shaft was excavated and the workings were drained by an engine installed at 46m. The bottom section of this upper seam contained balls of pyrites and was often left in place, while the 0.86-1.0m thick overlying coals were removed. Unfortunately the shaft for the engine pit went down very close to a fault, which had shattered much of the coal in its immediate surroundings, so that initially this coal was judged as of no more than moderate quality. At sites more distant from the shaft the coal quality improved, but it was difficult and expensive to work, having a 3.7m thick roof of weak shales, which required much timber for support. In this No. 2 Pit, the total thickness of the coals at any one locality decreased southwards from 0.94m to 0.71m in the northern half of the working to a few centimetres in the south. The dips decreased slightly, from one in four in the north to one in five in the south. In the northern end of the workings there were several small faults, which eventually cut out the coal.

When cutting an Air Pit mid-way between Pits Nos. 1 and 2 the shaft crossed three separate thin coals, but none of them was workable. Although 1.11m thick, the first was dominated by poor rough coals and little parrot coal was present. Its very weak roof would have required too much wood for supports. A second coal, 1.22m below was considered unworkable at a thickness of 0.46m, and a third coal 0.53m thick, a farther 3.66m below, contained some clay ironstone, but also had a weak and potentially dangerous roof. A borehole extending downwards for 33m below the base of the Air Pit encountered no more coals. At best, fifteen colliers worked the coals in summer and twenty in winter, when the local demand for coal was higher. In the southwestern part of the mine the working faces came together and in the north there was room for only eight or nine hewers. Output fell and the mine closed in 1863. Although trials were made of no less than four thin coals above the main parrot seam none was considered adequate for exploitation, despite the fact that the 'old people' were known to have worked the lowest and thickest of them.

Gemmell (1900) believed that the Parrot coal at Ladeddie was the equivalent of the combined Largoward Splint and Parrot coal worked at Denhead and Gowkston, and that the upper thick coals of Drumcarro should have reached the surface to the west of the Ladeddie steading if the dolerite sill had not displaced them. The area concerned lies north of one suggested line of the Ceres Fault zone, and an alternative site for the reappearance of the coal would be on the southern flank of Kinninmonth Hill, leading towards Nether Baldinnie. It is suggested that the persistent pyrites-rich layer, towards the base of the upper coals, may be a lateral equivalent of the banded ironstone horizons to the southeast and the Brassie Coal of the Radernie mines 4 km to the southeast. The lower coal is probably equivalent to the Low Little Coal of the Cassindonald area.

The Blackband Ironstones

The two coals in the Winthank-Denhead area were closely linked to the deposits of Blackband Ironstone which lay a short distance above the widely worked limestones of the Winthank district. The value of the ironstone, as a self-calcining ore, was not initially recognised in Fife, and much was cast aside as dross or waste material deposited in 'biggins' in abandoned rooms created when extracting the associated coals. However, according to an account in the Fifeshire Journal of 4th November 1847, when one of the Denhead colliers left to take up work in Lanarkshire, he recognised that the materials prized and being deliberately worked there were identical to those treated as rubbish in Fife. Indeed they had formed the basis of a new industry, following the lead of James Beaumont Neilson, then manager of the first gasworks in Glasgow, who patented his hot air blast furnace technique in 1828. The collier soon returned to Denhead and informed the proprietor, Mr Whyte Melville, who acted quickly to develop the new and very profitable industry, exporting the partly processed ores to furnaces in the north-east of England.

The uppermost part of the Blackband Ironstone was locally known as dunstane, a reference to the pale brown coloration of the iron carbonate minerals of which the rock is largely composed. Within it there are thin streaks of black material which often showed apparent floral patterns when split open along the bedding planes. This is a typical feature of rock weathering, with surface coatings of manganese oxides showing fractal-like patterns of deposition. The ironstone, reached its thickest at 0.71m at the eastern end of the lands of Cassindonald bordering the Winthank land of Mr. Anstruther Thomson, and became thinner into the Craigton Common grounds to the north and east, but again thickened towards Lumbo. Here at places it became almost unworkable due to a combination of folding and intense faulting in the fracture zones of the Maiden Rock and Ceres faults. In addition to a series of pre-1850 exploratory boreholes in the Lumbo area, the search for the ironstones continued and by 1866 had served to generate at least a dozen further, often deep bores, one reaching 110m. Several working pits were opened in the Lumbo area, using horse gins and windlass lifts. At least one steam engine is known to have operated here using locally mined coals to power the pumps. Many of the boreholes found the ironstones and associated coals, but there was little evidence of continuity of the structure of the rock succession as a result of the faulting. The Lochgelly Iron Company, Ltd, despite selling the calcined ores at 15/- per ton, found that it could not produce the raw ironstone at that price and abandoned the Lumbo works in 1858. At that time there was a depression in the price of iron in the market.

When, along the southern margins of the basin, Bulmer and Company traced the ironstone outcrop across Cassindonald grounds they found that the ore thinned westwards towards Wilkieston. The ironstone decreased in thickness to no more than a thin trace at Cassindonald, although the associated coals continued to be readily recognised, and no substantial ores were detected anywhere on the western outcrops of the coalfield.

The ore body extended northwards from Cassindonald to beyond the Winthank lands and was systematically extracted from beneath the Denhead section of the Craigton Common estate. Landale (1851) commented that Bell, who had worked originally on the ironstones of Thomson's land had moved to work those of Whyte Melville.

Most of the coals had been removed previously, leaving material only near faults. However, the ironstones remained, although they were not easy to work. A section of the rocks associated with the ironstones at Winthank and derived from records of the workings held by the National Mining Museum, Mansfield, is given in Fig. 18.

Some very minor workings of 1854 and 1855 shown on a Coal Authority plan extended below the eastern extremity of the grounds of Drumcarro. Landale (1847) had previously reported to Captain Holme Rigg of Tarvit that, despite repeated attempts, he had been unable to discover any surface outcrops of the ironstone either in the south-eastern parts of the lands of Drumcarro or on the flanks of the Drumcarrow Craigs. Mine working plans show that the ironstones were at least 36m below the surface at the eastern extremity of the Drumcarro grounds. After Bulmer had shown that the ironstone thinned away from Cassindonald, Sime worked the coals for a year, and later still, in 1875, Nicol and Edie, despite undertaking expensive surveys found nothing worth following in this area.

The initial ironstone mining operations involved reworking the former coal mine wastes to separate and recover the valuable ironstones, but mine abandonment plans in the archives of the Coal Authority show that, following a period of exploitation by opencast techniques, by 1849 the working panels had penetrated below ground from the eastern outcrop. Pre-existing pits were also used for access to the ironstones, and in 1848 at least two separate operations were under way, using shafts up to 37m deep. The workings penetrated progressively deeper towards the west and were noted by Forbes to have reached a maximum depth of 60m. By 1858, when the bulk of the exploitation had been completed to the south of the major east-west trending fault, fifteen individual shafts had been used, mostly arranged at spacings of 80-90m, reflecting the poor quality of the roofing layers to the ironstones. Mining to the north of the fault continued from a series of centres, but on a very reduced scale. The ironstone mines from Cassindonald to Winthank and Denhead, both north and south of the fault, were largely drained by a southward extension from the Gowkston Day Level.

The end of the working at Denhead was signalled in an advertisement of a displenishment roup to sell the mining plant from the working, on 7th September 1865. Items listed included iron pumps, pit rails, flat winding rope, winches, a pit head frame, bench, a wooden house and a large lot of bricks. In other accounts we learn that the tacksman was Nimmo, the works engineer was John Latto, possibly the former collier from Drumcarro, and the oversman was Thomas Ireland. In the Fife Herald News' the latter was reported as having made a presentation of a silver tea set to Mr. and Mrs. Nimmo in March 1857 at a meeting of the miners.

Once extracted, the ironstone was taken to open ground and broken into small pieces which were then arranged in piles with some coals. Small coals placed at the base of the heaps were set alight. The other coals within the heaps also ignited and within a few days the entire mass glowed, resembling a heated furnace. When cooled the remnants were substantially enriched in iron, but with greatly reduced carbonate contents. The ashes were separated and the iron concentrates taken to the harbours at St Andrews or Guardbridge for shipment to Newcastle. During this process of charring, or calcining the ore lost about a half of its weight. The treatment gave rise to about 400 tons of partly processed ore each week on which the royalty paid amounted to two shillings per ton. Landale estimated that each acre (0.4 ha) produced around 3000 calcined tons and yielded some £3000.

While seeking to stress the value of the ironstone deposits, Landale (1880) recalled that he had acted as adviser to the owners of each of the main three estates with interests in the ironstone mining from the lands of Craigton Common, namely Mr. Whyte Melville, Mr. Thomson and Mr. Rigg. He stated that in thirteen years of working from an area of 14 acres (5.7 ha) Mr Thomson's royalties amounted to £3768, and Mr. Melville's to twice as much, and where the ironstones were associated with workable coals the royalty value was even greater.

A number of proving boreholes were drilled for Bell but mysteriously they reached down only to the Five Foot (Mid-Kinniny) Limestone which is some 12.8m above the ironstones, suggesting that his interests were no longer in the ironstones, but had reverted to the limestones, which continued to be of commercial interest for their use in agriculture. A similar borehole in the grounds of Drumcarro, to the north, penetrated 42m before encountering the ironstones and coals which were reported to have become so denatured that they were too hard for the picks to work. This was due to the proximity of a dolerite sill about one metre below the coal. Neither the thin ironstones nor the coals could be worked at this site.

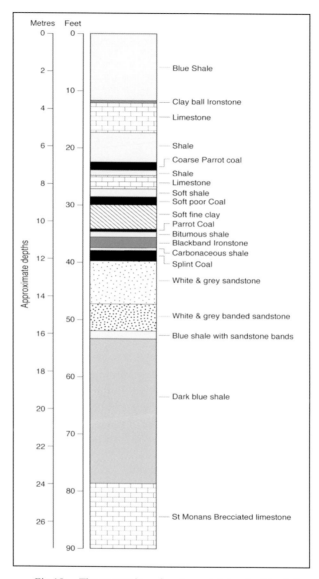

Fig.18.   The succession of rocks containing the Banded
Ironstone at the base of the Lower Limestone Formations
as exposed during opencast excavations at Winthank.
Information derived from Coal Authority map
Sheet No. S3575, dated 2007

Postscript

It is inevitable that the question will arise: 'Are there still viable reserves of coal to be found and exploited in this area of North East Fife?'

There are several sites where remnants of thick layers of coal remain in place, notably below the positions of the day levels, areas of thoroughly saturated ground which would require constant pumping to allow drainage. These are generally small pockets of coal, of very limited extent, often heavily faulted and intruded by igneous material. As such they would require costly investment in equipment for relatively little return and as a result are not seen as good economic prospects at the present time. None of these seams is at shallow enough depth to enable working in opencast mines.

There are certainly plenty of thin coal seams in the ground. Nobody today would wish to see colliers working in conditions considered unsuitable in the eighteenth and nineteenth centuries Even with the advanced forms of modern machinery these seams remain inaccessible. However, with the developments in clean coal technology for the production of gas and liquid hydrocarbons below ground without the release of climate-damaging gases, some of the smaller field residues might become of economic interest in the future.

Bibliography

Armstrong ,M. Chisholm, J.I. Forsyth, I.H. Paterson, I.B. Earp, J.R. Lawrie, T.R.M. and Poole, E.G. 1980. Arbroath. Geological Survey of Great Britain (Scotland), 1:50,000 scale Map 49.

Beaumont, F Report on the Ceres Coals. In Unpublished notes of S,B.Forbes, 1955 in the Library of the British Geological Survey, Murchison House Edinburgh.

Bennett, G.P.1978 The Past at work around the Lomonds. Markinch Printing Co, Markinch, 72pp.

Brodie, W.C.R. 1978-80 Introduction to the Rothes Papers. Proceedings of the Society of Antiquaries of Scotland. 110, 404-431.

Brotchie, A.W. 1998 The Wemyss Private Railway, The Oakwood Press.

Chisholm, J.I., Forsyth, I.H, Francis, E.H. and McAdam, A.D. 1970 North Berwick, Geological Survey of Great Britain (Scotland), 1;50,000 scale Map 41.

Cunningham, A.S. 1913 Mining in the Kingdom of Fife (2nd edition) Romanes & Son, Edinburgh. Minerals Planning Guidance. MPG3 Opencast Coal Mining.11pp

Duckham, Baron F., 1970 A History of the Scottish Coal Industry. Vol.1 1750-1815 David and Charles, Newton Abbot, 387pp.

Forbes, S.B. 1955 The coalfields of Fife. Unpublished MS National Coal Board 4 volumes, maps and sections, British Geological Survey Library, Edinburgh

Forsyth, I.H. and Chisholm J.I. 1968 Geological Survey boreholes in the Carboniferous of east Fife, 1963-4. Bulletin of the Geological Survey of Great Britain, No.28, 61-101.

Forsyth, I.H. and Chisholm J.I. 1977 The Geology of East Fife. Memoir of the Geological Survey of Great Britain, HMSO, Edinburgh, 284pp

Freese, B. 2006 Coal: a human history. Arrow Books, London, 337pp

Galloway, W. 1885, Report on the Pittenweem Coalfield. W.Lewis,

Cardiff. 7pp and maps.

Geikie, A. 1902 The Geology of Eastern Fife. Memoir of the Geological Survey of Great Britain 421pp.

Goodwin, R. 1959 Some physical and social factors in the evolution of a mining landscape. Scottish Geographical Magazine, 75, 3-17.

Halliday, R.S. 1990. The disappearing Scottish Colliery. Scottish Academic Press, Edinburgh, 199pp.

Hutton, G. 1999 Fife: the Mining Kingdom. Stanlake Publishing, Ochiltree, Ayrshire. 112Pp

King, L. 2001 Sair, Sair Wark: Women and mining in Scotland. Windfall Books, Kelty, 134pp.

Landale, D. 1835 Reports on part of the coal district situated between the Forth and the Tay. Transactions of the Royal Highland Agricultural Society, X, 410-439.

Landale, D. 1837 Report on the Geology of the East Fife Coalfield with map and sections. Transactions of the Royal Highland Agricultural Society, XI, 265-348

MacGregor, A.R. 1968 Fife & Angus Geology: an excursion guide. 1968. Blackwood & Sons Ltd, Edinburgh, 266.

McKechnie, J & Macgregor, M. 1958 A short history of the Scottish Coalmining Industry. National Coal Board, Scottish Division, 116pp.

McManus, J. 2008 Impacts of Coal Mining and Abandonment. *In* C.A.Galbraith and J.M.Baxter Energy and the environment. Scottish Natural Heritage, The Stationery Office, Edinburgh, 21-32.

Martin, C. 1999 The 18th century industrial landscape between St Monans and Pittenweem: a cartographic and archaeological study. *In* P.Yeoman (Ed.)The salt and coal industries of St Monans, Fife in the 18th and 19th centuries. Tayside and Fife Archaeological Committee, Glenrothes, 42-66.

Martin, M.2002 www.users.zetnet.co.uk/fifepits/east/images/maps/mapb12. jpg

Martin, P. 1999 The Newark Coal and Salt Work Company, its social and economic impact. In P.Yeoman (Ed.)The salt and coal industries of St Monans, Fife in the 18th and 19th centuries. Tayside and Fife Archaeological Committee, Glenrothes, 28-41

Melville, J. 1793 The Banfield Coal Book, Unpublished accounts. Cupar, Fife Reference Library.

Montgomery, G. 1994 A mining chronicle. Newcraighall Heritage Society, Musselburgh, 328pp.

Moodie, D.M.2002 A dark and dismal strife. Dauv. Miner Publications, Grantully, Perthshire, 599pp.

Muir, A. 1958 The Fife Coal Company: A short history. The Fife Coal Company Ltd, Leven. 133pp.

Muirhead, G. 1792 Statistical Account of Scotland : Dysart. 12, 502-504.

Parliamentary Commission on the Employment of Children in Mines. First Report,1842, 2131pp.

Payne, P.L. 1982 The Halbeath Colliey and Saltworks, 1785-91 In A.Slaven & D.H.Aldcroft (Eds.) Business, Banking, and Urban History, Scottish Academic Press, Edinburgh, 1-33.

The details of the many unpublished Mining Engineer reports from the quoted authors are to be found in the unpublished collation report by Forbes, located in the library of the British Geological Survey, at Murchison House, West Mains Road,

APPENDIX 1

Glossary of terms used by the mining industry

Biggin - a build up of wastes from the coal workings into worked rooms

Bing – a heap of coal debris or colliery waste.

Blaes - mudstone or shale with little bituminous or carbonaceous matter, but enough to give a dark blue-grey colour to the rock

Blind coal - coal which has been partly carbonised and effectively destroyed by its proximity to an igneous intrusion

Brushings - rocks above or below a worked seam which are removed in constructing and maintaining access roads.

Calm - pale coloured blaes, often developed near an igneous intrusion. Where hardened and bleached these were formerly used as slate pencils.

Cannel - (formerly candle coal) - lustreless coal which yields much gas and gives a long lasting bright flame

Chain - a measure of length consisting of one hundred brass links with ten intervening markers. A chain Scots was 74 feet long. The Imperial chain is 66 feet in length.

Cherry coal - bright, lustrous, freely burning coal, good for domestic use.

Craw coal - a poor coal usually in a thin seam often a short distance above a major coal, and so serves as an indicator

Daugh - soft, coaly fireclay which may be above, within or below a coal seam.

Dip - inclination of the layering from the horizontal, quoted as an angle or as a gradient.

Dyke - steeply inclined sheet of igneous rock which cuts across the layers of sedimentary rocks

Fakes - thin bedded muddy sandstone or sandy mudstone

Fathom – a measure of depth or distance. One fathom is six feet.

Fault - a fracture plane along which the rock succession is displaced.

Free coal -easily broken coal which burns readily

Goaf (Goaves) - waste material below ground from an area of a mined coal seam

Holing - removal of a thin layer of soft material close to a seam, often beneath, before removing the coal.

Kingle - very hard rock, usually sandstone with silica or carbonate cement

Level - a main drainage and roadway leading horizontally past galleries or rooms from which coal excavation takes place.

March dyke - the wall marking the boundary between two neighbouring estates.

Mine a) - a drift or roadway sloping from the surface
     b) - a drift from an underground seam which cuts across strata, usually   towards another seam (cross-cut or stone mine)

Parrot coal - a rather inferior coal used for gas making. Chatters and spits when burned

Parting - a plane along which a uniform rock type is subdivided into separate layers

Pavement - the rock layer immediately beneath a coal seam

Pelt - a bituminous shale, often bearing some plant material
Ply - a solid layer of hard rock separated from its neighbours by partings
Plies - rapid alternations of hard and soft layers of rock
Rib - a thin layer of hard material
Roof - the rock layer immediately above a worked coal seam
Rough coal - a name sometimes applied to free coal as against splint or cannel
Sclit - shaly coal or coaly blaes
Shale - laminated mudstone
Sill - a body of igneous rock which is gently inclined or mainly parallel to the layering.
Splint coal - hard coal with low lustre, and grainy texture, which breaks unevenly and
        does not easily crush in a blast furnace or during transport.
Stoop and Room - method of working coal by extracting galleries or rooms separated
        by broad pillars or stoops.
Trouble - feature such as a fault or dyke interrupting working of a coal seam
Waste - rubble from old workings
Whin or Whinstone or Greenstone - hard darkly coloured igneous rock usually
        present in Fife as sills or dykes.
Working - name given to the rocks disturbed to excavate a coal seam.

APPENDIX 2

Throughout the text reference has been made to exploratory boreholes. For each borehole a log showing the succession of rocks types encountered at the various depths below the surface. The quality of the logs varies greatly according to the experience of the driller. Nevertheless, all could recognise coal when they found it. The depths determined were approximate. Some examples of early borehole logs recorded in the journals of Thomson and Cochrane at Callange and Kinninmonth are given below. Unfortunately the precise locations of the bores are not known.

Thomson's Journals
No 1(a) 23 fathoms 3ft 3 inches (141ft 3in) deep and got nothing, it being a foolish site begun at the coal formation.
No.1 (b) **Kinninmonth** 32 fathoms (192ft) deep ending in 1ft 4.5ins limestone, having got no coal.
No 2 (c) **Kinninmonth** Got an 18 inch coal at 12 fathoms (72ft) from the surface and 13ft under it the journal shows a coal 4ft 5ins thick with a remark that it is a good workable thickness. This bore got no further coals to 25 fathoms (150ft).
No.1 (d) **Callange** down 36.5 fathoms (219ft) in a poor bore and no workable thing in it.
No.2(c) **Callange** down 10 fathoms (60ft), the coal 4.5 feet being in whinstone, quite unpromising.

Cochrane's Borehole Journals

No.1 bore passes through the same strata as the going pit. Commences on the pavement of the upper coal, got coal at 35 fathoms 3ft 3ins (213ft 3in) in the journal, but it is 33 fathoms (198ft) in the pit.
No. 2 bore got no coal, it being in rotten whinstone.
No. 3 at 3 fathoms (18ft) deep the rods went through an old coal waste 6ft 9 ins under a hitch.
No. 4 bored 6.5 fathoms (39ft) in rotten whin rock
BH 5 passed through a 14inch coal at 10 fathoms (60ft) deep- no use.
BH 6 23 fathoms deep (138ft) passed through a 5 inch coal near the bottom
BH 7 close to Coaltown of Callange passed through the upper coal 2ft 9 ins thick at 9ft from the surface. At 25 fathoms (150ft) it passd through a limestone 27 ins thick and through the second coal at 39 fathoms (234 ft). This bore was carried on 29 fathoms (to 354ft) and passed through a foul coal of no use 14 inches thick which gave much water and it is this one which was plugged up after the drowning of the colliery workings.
BH 8 was in troubled ground- all the metals being foul. At 8 fathoms (48ft) it passed through a foul coal 5ft thick and a 14inch band of pyrites at 14 fathoms (84ft)

List of Text-figures

Fig.1.   Original workings gave access to coals in section A, above the natural water table. Construction of the day level tunnel to lower the water table provided access to coals in section B.

Fig.2.   A section across a bell pit with access by way of three ladders.   The coals were worked radially from the shaft base, with waste materials being left behind. Wooden props supported the roof above the coal seam.

Fig.3.   Illustration of 'stoop and room' or 'pillar and stall' method of extraction. Much coal was left in place to support the roof of the workings.

Fig.4.   Plan of the former workings between Pittenweem and St Monans, after Galloway (1895). The residual coal pillars are indicated in black. The levels in the Fore Coal and Parrot Coal drained to 38 fathoms, the waters were raised at the Engine Pit, and discharged at the 'mineral well'.

Fig.5   Longwall working, in which all of the coals are progressively removed, and as the working face retreats down slope the roof undergoes controlled collapse as hydraulic props are sequentially removed.

Fig.6.   Horizon mining, in which horizontal stone mines are driven to provide access to several coal seams from the one roadway. The coals are worked up the slope of the seam.

Fig.7.   Map of the Denhead syncline showing the outcrops of the Black and Parrot Coals and a cross-section to show the basin-like profile. The dotted line marks the position of the Gowkston day level, and the numbers indicate known site of the air shafts leading to it. (after McLaren, 1822).

Fig.8   Geological Map of the eastern coalfields, based on information from Ballingal, Landale, Forbes, Pinshon, Gemmel, the British Geological Survey, and personal observations.

Fig.9   Bodies of igneous rocks arising from a magmatic source. Sills are parallel to the layering or inclined at low angles. Dykes are near vertical or steeply inclined, are often intruded along pre-existing faults..

Fig.10   The coal seams of the Ceres White Den gradually steepen northwards. Both surface outcrop working and extraction from day level tunnels was normal here, with access shafts arranged above the level tunnels. The position of Coal Road is indicated.

Fig.11   Three dimensional representation of the form of workings in the early 18th Century.

Fig.12.   The two levels of working the Callange Coals in 1775.

Fig 13. Sketch of coal workings at Mount Melville, (after Landale)

Fig.14.   Plans of the Denork mines as surveyed by Landale (1889), showing the principal working roads in (a) Coal A, the Scrumpie Coal, and (b) Coal C.   The inserted cross section indicates the eastward dipping seams and the relative positions of the workings.

Fig.15 A northwest to southeast cross-section of the western Drumcarro workings indicating levels to which the coals had been worked from the surface, the Crop Pit, the Old Engine Pit and the Engine Pit. Note the decreasing dip of the coal seams with depth (after Landale, 1841). The thicknesses of the seams are not shown to scale.

Fig.16   Geological map of the Backfield of Ladeddie coalfield, after Ballingal (in MacLean 1818).

Fig.17 Plan of the two workings operating to the southeast of Ladeddie steading in the period 1858-1863.

Fig.18.   The succession of rocks containing the Banded Ironstone at the base of the Lower Limestone Formation as exposed during opencast excavations at Winthank. Information derived from Coal Authority map Sheet No. S3575, dated 2007.